GARDENING
IN A CHANGING CLIMATE

GARDENING
IN A CHANGING CLIMATE

Inspirational and practical ideas for creating sustainable, waterwise and dry
gardens, with projects, garden plans and more than 400 photographs

Ambra Edwards

with special photography by Lynn Keddie

aqua marine

This edition is published by Aquamarine, an imprint of Anness Publishing Ltd, Hermes House, 88–89 Blackfriars Road, London SE1 8HA; tel. 020 7401 2077; fax 020 7633 9499

www.aquamarinebooks.com; www.annesspublishing.com

If you like the images in this book and would like to investigate using them for publishing, promotions or advertising, please visit our website www.practicalpictures.com for more information.

UK distributor: Book Trade Services; tel. 0116 2759086; fax 0116 2759090; uksales@booktradeservices.com; exportsales@booktradeservices.com
North American distributor: National Book Network; tel. 301 459 3366; fax 301 429 5746; www.nbnbooks.comAustralian distributor: Pan Macmillan Australia; tel. 1300 135 113; fax 1300 135 103; customer.service@macmillan.com.au
New Zealand distributor: David Bateman Ltd; tel. (09) 415 7664; fax (09) 415 8892

Publisher: Joanna Lorenz
Editorial Director: Helen Sudell
Project Editor: Emma Clegg
Designer: Simon Daley
Jacket Design: Lisa Tai
Special photography: Lynn Keddie, with additional photographs by Stephen Wooster and Peter Anderson
Illustrator: Liz Pepperell
Production Controller: Wendy Lawson

Page 1: The South African natives knifphofia and agapanthus carry the garden's brilliant colours right through to the end of the summer.

Page 2: The wall of this Córdoban patio garden houses a mass of sun-loving pelargoniums; water them with a soaker hose or by drip irrigation, methods that ensure the most economical use of water.

Page 3: The drought-tolerant *Allium hollandicum* 'Purple Sensation', also known as ornamental onion, loves a spot in the full sun.

ETHICAL TRADING POLICY
Because of our ongoing ecological investment programme, you, as our customer, can have the pleasure and reassurance of knowing that a tree is being cultivated on your behalf to replace the materials used to make the book you are holding. For further information about this scheme, go to www.annesspublishing.com/trees

A CIP catalogue record for this book is available from the British Library.

Bracketed terms are intended for American readers.

In the United States, throughout the Sun Belt states, from Florida, across the Gulf Coast, southern Texas, southern deserts to southern California and coastal regions, annuals are planted in the autumn, bloom in the winter and spring, and die at the beginning of summer.

PUBLISHER'S NOTE
Although the advice and information in this book are believed to be accurate and true at the time of going to press, neither the authors nor the publisher can accept any legal responsibility or liability for any errors or omissions that may have been made nor for any inaccuracies nor for any loss, harm or injury that comes about from following instructions or advice in this book.

Main cover image reproduced courtesy of Jonathan Need/Gap Photos.

Contents

Introduction

If more politicians had been gardeners, the reality of climate change would have been acknowledged years ago. All of us, in all parts of the world, have seen the seasons alter, flowering times advance, growing seasons last longer, and combinations of plants as old as folk memory unravel and reform anew. So how exactly should we help our gardens adapt?

Changing patterns

Earlier snowmelts are threatening montane plant communities across the globe, as alpines burst into bejewelled flower weeks before their pollinators are active. In Britain, the primroses, harbingers of spring, now regularly appear in the autumn, while in New England, rising temperatures are causing the fall to arrive earlier and less vividly. We are told that the biggest change will be felt in the temperate areas of the northern hemisphere, such as northern Europe and North America.

To begin with, some of us didn't mind too much. Gardeners in northern Europe could view with equanimity the prospect of shorter, milder winters, and summers as balmy as the south of France. Urban gardeners started growing olives in their sheltered backyards.

But Californian gardeners soon found that winter snows falling as rain meant more acute water shortage in summer. Greece, Florida and Australia – all regions accustomed to drought and summer wildfires – experienced both on an unimaginable scale. We simply hadn't bargained for the extremes of weather that global warming would bring – heatwaves and hosepipe bans, wild summer storms, torrential rain and floods, let alone hurricanes and infernos. Looking at the wreckage of our gardens (and sometimes our homes), it became clear that climate change was more complex than we thought.

Those milder winters might mean fewer frosts, but we now know they will be increasingly wet – and few plants are well disposed to waterlogging. With no cold snaps to see them off, we can expect higher levels of pest and disease. With less rain falling in summer (despite more rain overall), and higher summer temperatures, summer drought will become commonplace. Increased levels of carbon dioxide will mean plants mature earlier, and grow faster. But other plants – ones that need a season of cold to develop – won't grow at all.

How are our traditional lawns and flower borders to cope with all this?

Suddenly, it is clear to see, a style of gardening that has endured for 150 years or more, has been overtaken by events.

Facing the challenge

Of course, climate change is not a new phenomenon. It has occurred many times in the earth's history. This current phase of global warming has been going on since the mid-19th century. But what is different this time round is the speed of the transformation – a warming rate of 0.1–0.3°C (0.18–0.5°F) per decade – far too fast for plant adaptation. Average temperatures worldwide are now predicted to rise by up to 5.8°C (12°F) by 2100, almost twice previous estimates. And we already know that changes of only a fraction of one degree are sufficient to trigger major changes in weather patterns.

These stark facts set us a challenge – to think about gardening in a new way. This book is a small, tentative step in that direction. It is an invitation to see what we can learn from other countries, and other cultures, for whom heat, and drought, and water-shortage have always been facts of life. Are there styles or elements of gardens we can adapt for our own use? With an uncertain future, there are undoubtedly useful lessons to be found in the past. The great sun-drenched gardens of Italy or the oasis gardens of Islam, for example, offer two fine models.

Opposite
Milder winters and hotter summers offer us the chance to experiment with a wider palette of plants, such as these lovely South African red hot pokers.

Above
Bananas, palms, cacti and bromeliads offer a new plant vocabulary for the modern urban garden.

borders in the 1880s. These days, who has time for scarifying and top-dressing, for staking and daily deadheading? It is time to move on.

Yes, there will be terrible losses. English beechwoods, Chinese magnolias, American prairie orchids – all are under threat. How will gardeners fare without the blackcurrant, when winters are too warm for it to bear fruit? What will cottage gardens look like without lupins and delphiniums, asters and phlox? But there will also be fantastic opportunities in our new, warmer, sunnier gardens. Gardeners in temperate Europe have only to look to Australia and New Zealand, the Mediterranean and South Africa, to discover a stupendous range of exciting plants that will thrive in these warmer temperatures – many little known to us as yet. Desert gardens in Arizona, gravel gardens in Japan, historic gardens in Italy – all show how tough conditions can produce gardens of astonishing beauty.

For the climates already supporting these plant species, there will also be new challenges. The first is to respond creatively to their own shifting weather patterns. (In Australia, for example, the last 50 years have seen reduced rainfall in the south, with summer heatwaves and warmer winters in the east.) The second challenge is to embrace within the garden a native flora that has perhaps been under-appreciated, and which may also be threatened by alien invaders such as agapanthus in New Zealand or the Australian wattles that are displacing South Africa's unique fynbos flora. Species with fast generation times and wide ecological tolerances are better equipped to deal with rapid climate change than species with long generation times or specific habitat requirements, such as alpines, forest trees or the proteas of the Cape; these plants urgently need safe havens.

Everywhere, the world's plants are faced with three bleak options: to adapt to the new environmental conditions, to find more appropriate ones by migrating to higher altitudes or latitudes, or simply to die out. When an estimated one-quarter of vascular plant species are threatened with extinction in the wild, gardeners have a vital role to play in preserving biodiversity.

Above all, it is a call to gardeners to do what we have always done best – to respond to an ever-changing natural world with resourcefulness and creativity. Our verdant lawns and multi-layered herbaceous borders may have had their day, but that day has been a long one. Mr Budding patented his lawnmower in 1833; summer bedding was a response to technological changes in the mid-19th century, while Gertrude Jekyll designed her first colour

Adapting to climate change won't always be easy. Drought-tolerant plants that love scorching summers won't like winter wet – meaning many hours' investment in good drainage. Hard landscaping will have to be more porous, and better able to cope with flash flooding. And we must all think about gardening more sustainably – restricting the use of power tools, using local materials, composting and recycling, water harvesting and mulching, throwing away pesticides and relearning traditional cultivation techniques.

This book shows you how to start to address the challenge of climate change in your own backyard. It investigates nine garden styles that have always dealt superbly with heat, drought or water shortage, or all three. Some, such as The Mediterranean Garden and The Patio Garden, have familiar elements. Others, such as The Cape Garden and The Jungle Garden, offer new planting palettes for flora that was once exclusive to certain regions. Each chapter first explores the visual splendour of the style, and then shows how to create the features and select the plants – with a practical tutorial, a plant focus, a planting plan and a step-by-step project. A plant directory paints a vivid picture of each entry and explains the practicalities of its growth and cultivation.

We can't pretend the challenge will be easy. But with so much to learn, and with so many enticing new plants within our grasp, there has never been a more exciting time to be a gardener.

Below
A sustainable garden need not be an austere one – as shown by this Mediterranean-style garden with its exuberant use of wild flowers.

The Italianate garden

The sunny gardens of Italy are outdoor rooms in which to relax, to entertain friends, to eat, chat and play. The outdoor room is an ancient idea – as far back as 100AD the Roman official Pliny the Younger described his garden as a place to escape the city and sit in the sunshine, fanned by cool breezes, enjoying a delightful view. Indoors and outdoors merged into one, in a series of porticos, courtyards and colonnades. Vines were trained to shade a curving dining seat, where, during banquets, dishes floated in bird-shaped vessels in a marble basin.

For centuries, the Italian garden has been the starting point for every formal garden, with its emphasis on structure, symmetry and perspective. While these gardens were invariably grand, with stepped levels and spectacular water features, other aspects of the style offer a blueprint for the modern garden. Especially attractive are the tough plants that survive the various conditions of a climate in change. So let us welcome the fast-growing and resilient evergreens, the elegant sculptural forms of topiary and statuary and the shade-giving vines.

Opposite
The distinctive elements of the Italianate garden – symmetry, architectural stonework and extensive use of evergreen topiary – can be transported to many different countries and types of space. Iford Manor, for example, is a famous Italianate garden created on a verdant hillside in England.

Above left
While mythical beings are often subjects of garden sculpture, a favourite pet will do just as well.

Above right
This richly carved sarcophagus shows how decorative stonework is integrated in a classical garden.

The gardens of the cardinals

The letters of Pliny, along with other classical texts, formed the inspiration for the great gardens of the Italian Renaissance, created in the 15th and 16th centuries by princes, cardinals and popes. Guided by these literary sources, they built shady loggias, vine-covered pergolas and arbours to retreat to in the heat of the day. They filled their gardens with water, in pools and canals, cascades and fountains. Instead of the enclosed gardens of the medieval period, they favoured gardens on hillsides which they opened to the view and cooling breezes, exploiting the steepness of the site to create a sequence of terraces, linked by magnificent ramps or staircases, and adorned

with noble balustrades, classical statuary (often raided from Roman sites) and decorative garden buildings.

These were sociable spaces, designed to be shared. The earliest were outdoor salons, where friends met to exchange philosophical ideas. Over time, they became more grandiose, intended to impress upon the visitor the wealth and power of their owners. Al fresco dining became something of an art form: at the Villa Lante in Bagnaia, for example, a chute of water that forms the principal axis of the garden is channelled at mid-point through a long dining table of stone, where it filled a trough to cool the cardinal's wine. Other gardens had outdoor

Above
At Castello Ruspoli, in Lazio, the garden remains unchanged from 1610. Lemon trees in pots line the paths, a fountain plays at the centre, while elaborate box parterres spell out the initials of the garden creator.

theatres to entertain their guests, or elaborate waterworks, or mysterious grottoes. But as gardens grew increasingly ostentatious, the idea of a secret retreat became ever more appealing. A *giardino segreto* or secret garden might be concealed behind a high hedge – a haven of tranquillity away from the pomp and circumstance of the garden beyond.

These sunny villa gardens were to inspire countless imitations through the centuries, from the elegant parterres of the French Baroque to the Getty villa in Malibu. The style enjoyed a huge revival in the mid-19th and again in the early 20th century throughout Britain, America and Europe, fuelled by enthusiastic writers such as Edith Wharton (1862–1937).

At Trentham, England, in 1840, Sir Charles Barry (1795–1860), architect of London's Houses of Parliament, created the first of a series of swaggering Italianate gardens, using staircases, balustrading, urns and statuary, fountains and loggias. In Florida, USA, the Villa Vizcaya (1912–16)

blended ideas (and artefacts) from Verona, Venice and Rome. In Britain, Ireland and the south of France, designer Harold Peto (1854–1933) developed a poetic Italianate style, swathing Renaissance-inspired villas with swags of roses, and creating at his own home at Iford Manor in England, an exquisite setting for his collection of Roman and Renaissance art. In Italy, meanwhile, an influx of wealthy English and Americans began restoring neglected historic gardens, and creating new Italian ones of their own.

Today, perhaps, it is the earlier gardens which offer the most powerful inspiration for our own gardens. Although many were conceived on a massive scale, the strength and simplicity of their layouts offer a surprisingly effective way of dealing with our own small urban spaces. The theatricality of Italian design suggests a way to make even a tiny courtyard dramatic and interesting. And wherever we garden, there are features we can borrow from the villa garden to make vivid and enjoyable outdoor rooms.

Below left
The 16th-century stone dining table at the Villa Lante, Bagnaia, with inbuilt wine cooler. Two more channels beneath the table would cool the toes of the Cardinal and his guests.

Below right
The Renaissance garden was intended to offer a peaceful haven from the stresses and strains of city life. The tranquil beauty of Iford Manor, with its romantic loggias, sweeping stairways and magnificent rural views, perfectly captures this spirit.

Garden architecture

The gardeners of Renaissance Italy were the first to understand the garden in terms of geometry, applying mathematical rules of harmony and proportion to garden layout, as to the built environment. Their skilful use of symmetry and perspective remain the building blocks for all formal gardens to this day.

Manipulating space

The key feature of Italian Renaissance gardens was a central axis leading from the house, intersected at right angles by cross axes. These divided the space into a series of garden rooms, usually arranged symmetrically in a sequence of terraces, and linked by staircases, ramps and cascades. Lines of perspective (a new and exciting discovery) were emphasized with lines of trees, clipped topiary, or decorative stonework. The object was to achieve not only a harmonious whole, but unity between house and garden, and between the garden and the wider environment.

This is an excellent starting point for any garden. Even the smallest will benefit from being divided into several distinct spaces. And the smaller the garden, the more important it is to use strong, simple shapes – squares, rectangles, circles or semi-circles – and to think of the space as a sculptural whole. By manipulating the space, we can actually change the way we perceive its dimensions. For example, leading the eye to a focal point along a path or avenue will make the plot seem longer; while dividing it horizontally will make it seem wider. This effect can be exaggerated by cheating the perspective – by narrowing a path or avenue as it moves away from the viewpoint, we can make the end of a vista seem further away than it actually is.

A good place to begin is to divide the garden into foreground (perhaps your patio or terrace), middle ground, and background: think how you might distinguish them, and what points of interest you need in each section. If you have room and time to spare, there is no more pleasing way of dividing a garden than by living walls of evergreen hedging. Hornbeam and yew both make excellent hedges – and yew is not as slow as is generally supposed. The secret of fast growth is to prepare the ground well, and water religiously for the first two years. In successive years watering should only be necessary in hot and dry conditions. If a hedge is not feasible, trelliswork panels, painted or curtained with foliage, provide an effective and inexpensive alternative.

Below
The hornbeam tunnel has many uses – it can divide the garden space, lead to a focal point, or provide welcome shelter from hot sun or prying eyes.

Three-dimensional gardening

A change of level always adds interest to a garden. On a flat site, consider a raised or sunken area – even a small (15cm/6in) step will make all the difference. But on a steeply sloping site, the Italian approach turns difficulty into opportunity. Slopes are hard to manage, while few plants appear to advantage. Sculpting the slope into a series of terraces, though expensive at the outset, will reward you with easier maintenance. Make the terraces, and the steps that link them, as wide as you can: an over-generous proportion is easier on the eye than a mean one.

Think about the possibilities offered by the vertical surfaces in your garden – for evergreen climbers such as ivy, jasmine, or glossy-leaved *Trachelospermum jasminoides*. If you are lucky enough to have a warm, sunny wall, espaliered pears or fan-trained fruit such as apricots or peaches are not only delicious, but highly ornamental.

Try to include at least one three-dimensional feature such as a pergola, arch or arbour. In the Italian garden, a vine-clad pergola was vital to escape the sun. In the modern town garden, it offers shade and privacy from your neighbours, and vines will thrive in the sheltered microclimate. A pergola draped in plants provides a shady walk, and can be used to divide the space and to create a sense of journey. A favourite feature was a leafy tunnel of interlocking branches: a marvellous modern example can be seen at the Alnwick Garden in the north of England. Vertical accents can also be provided by individual plants – and none is more elegant, or gives better value for the ground space it uses, than the soaring Italian cypress (*Cupressus sempervirens*).

Above left
A steeply sloping site can appear a problem. But here, the space is divided into a series of narrow terraces, linked by a grand staircase at one end of the garden. The openings on to the terraces, marked by the piers, are also narrow, creating a sense of mystery and surprise.

Above right
A vine-clad pergola creates a private space at the end of this garden, a place to relax in dappled shade, and a delicious crop of grapes.

Green and serene

Part of the Italian garden's enduring appeal is its simplicity, depending as it does on a limited palette of drought-tolerant, evergreen plants. These plants, however, offer unending scope in the garden, in their variety of colour, texture and form, from hornbeam, box and ivy to cypress and bay.

Evergreens for hedges and topiary

Only drought-tolerant shrubs and trees could survive the hot Italian summer, and most of these are evergreen, with no dormant period. So the garden values form above colour, key plants being densely growing evergreens such as box, sweet bay (*Laurus nobilis*), Portugal laurel (*Prunus lusitanica*), myrtle (*Myrtus communis*) and yew, clipped into hedges and decorative shapes. Topiary is the most ancient of garden arts: Roman gardens sported leafy people, animals and letters. It is also the most universal, as much at home in a cottage garden as a princely pleasure ground.

Gardening with evergreens has many benefits: the all-green palette is restful and harmonious; it associates well with architecture, bringing an air of distinction to the simplest urban courtyard; while the planting is low-maintenance and provides interest and structure throughout the year. While some traditional Italian choices, like myrtle and phyllirea, need a warm climate, there are many hardier options, like box and yew.

Creating definition and shape

The Italian garden shows us that there is no end to the beauty and versatility of evergreen plants – dividing and linking space with living walls, arches and arcardes; emphasizing the garden's geometry with repeated forms – balls, pyramids, or slender columns of green; or tracing out elaborate patterns in low hedge parterres or mazes. While a maze may not be a viable feature, defining a space with crisp box hedges, or introducing rhythm by repeating forms, such as topiary cones, is easily achievable.

Opposite
This garden demonstrates the variety of colour and texture that evergreens can provide, with hedges of box, standards of bay and a stilt hedge of pleached hornbeam. New growing and cutting techniques mean that simple topiary shapes are widely available and affordable – or you can create them yourself.

Tutorial | Making framed ivy topiary

The beauty of ivy topiary is that you can achieve a complete form relatively quickly. Ivy-covered frames work well in pots and are ideal for the smaller garden. Select plain green ivy plants, preferably those with long stems. Pick a variety of ivy that has short 'joints' or internodes (the space between the buds) because this will produce compact growth with a good coverage.

1 Push the frame into position and plant the ivies around the pot rim so that the stems are next to the base of the frame.

2 Wind the stems of the ivy plants around the upright struts – the leaf bases act like grappling hooks. Try to create an even coverage.

3 As the plants grow, spread out the new shoots until the frame is covered. Trim off any excess foliage to maintain the spiral shape. Feed regularly.

Atmospheric essentials

The simple geometric bones and understated planting of the Italian garden are brought to life with sparkling water and carefully chosen statuary. No Italian garden is complete without a statue or urn to act as a focal point, and a fountain to bring light and movement to the scene.

The decorated garden

A harmonious pairing of clipped greenery and elegant stonework is the very essence of the Italian garden. Many villa gardens were designed as outdoor galleries, to show off lavish collections of statuary. At La Pietra, in Florence, the garden was made as a backdrop for an eclectic collection of over 200 statues. At Iford Manor in Wiltshire, the garden is decorated with all kinds of artefacts, from classical busts to bronze deer, and marble wellheads to sarcophagi; while the Capponi family of Florence commissioned statues of their favourite dogs. But a single shapely urn is all it takes to create the flavour of an Italian garden. Tiny city courtyards can be furnished with outsize urns, creating just that playful sense of theatre beloved by the Renaissance princes. The Italians thought of their gardens as stage sets, as delightful backdrops for

Below left
A well-chosen statue or pot makes a fine focal point. Giant urns can be used to create drama amd delight in a tiny courtyard.

Below right
If a classical nymph or river god seems out of place in the modern garden, try a favourite animal for ornament.

human activity, so your garden should never feel solemn. An authentically Italianate garden has a lively sense of fun.

Good paving is essential, and where natural stone is too expensive, there are now acceptable concrete imitations. Modern concrete versions of statuary and balustrading, however, should be treated with caution. At the very least, their stark white will need toning down, by painting with yogurt to encourage algal growth, or dousing with muddy water. They will also need careful placing: the balustrade copied from the terrace of a palace may look ill-at-ease in a humble suburban garden. Terracotta pots, however, look well everywhere, and can be grouped to make attractive focal points in the garden. They also offer the opportunity to introduce seasonal colour – or if you wish to hit a more authentic note, plant them up with fragrant orange or lemon trees.

Water, water everywhere

The Renaissance garden rejoiced in sophisticated water features: there were water-powered organs and singing birds, water parterres and innumerable fountains. The garden-makers particularly delighted in *giochi d'aqua* – hidden water jets that would suddenly drench unsuspecting visitors.

While we are all aware of the need to use it wisely, nothing brings a garden to life like water. Where space is at a premium, a wall-mounted fountain may be the solution, while even the tiniest reflecting pool will bring light and refreshment into the garden. A simple jet in a circular pool makes a marvellous centrepiece for any formal layout. All these features can be made with concealed reservoirs and recirculating pumps. Greywater recycling systems and solar-powered fountains are also available.

Above left
A simple chute of water into a tank brings animation and light to a shady spot.

Above right
Water jets shoot up from bowls set into a low box hedge in this elaborate garden feature. But even a single jet from a simple circular pool will charge the garden with energy and movement.

Plant focus Italian classics

These plants have been lynchpins of the Italian garden since Roman times, and still remain so today. Choose box for structure, cypress for impact, and lemons and vines for fragrance and ornament. All will bring an instant flavour of Italy to your garden.

Vitis vinifera

Buxus sempervirens   *Cupressus sempervirens*

Cupressus sempervirens Italian cypress
Perhaps the most characteristic plant of the Italian garden is the slender, pencil-like cypress, which provides an elegant punctuation point in any formal scheme. *C. s.* 'Pyramidalis' is the variety most commonly offered. It requires a sheltered site with excellent drainage. In more exposed gardens, the effect can be replicated with *Juniperus scopulorum* 'Skyrocket' or 'Blue Arrow', which are more resistant to frost and scorching winds. (See also page 140.)

Buxus sempervirens Common box
This is the ultimate topiary plant – a vigorous shrub or small tree with luxuriant masses of small, dark green foliage, and a curious earthy aroma. Many of the species originate from limestone regions, but box will tolerate any type of soil, as long as it is adequately drained in winter, and will grow in sun or shade. In very hot conditions, regular watering will stop the leaves from scorching. *B. sempervirens* is best for taller hedges; *B. s.* 'Suffruticosa' is a slower growing cultivar suitable for parterres and small hedges; while *B. microphylla* is a naturally compact form of box that needs virtually no clipping. (See also page 140.)

Citrus limon flowers

Citrus limon

Vitis vinifera Grape vine
The beautiful dappled shade it casts is enough to justify the vine's place in the garden – the grapes are a bonus! Although they are hardy, vines will ripen their crop most successfully in areas where summers are long and warm, and will benefit from a sheltered, sunny site. Most vines in Europe are derived from *Vitis vinifera*. *V. v.* 'Siegerebbe' is a good dual-purpose variety producing sweet, green, Muscat-like fruit. For black grapes choose *V.* 'Brant' – with lovely, five-lobed, fresh green leaves, which turn rich red and orange in autumn, and prolific (if pippy) fruit. In colder regions, go for 'Concord', a cultivated form of *Vitis labrusca*, and the most widely grown in the USA. (See also page 143.)

Citrus limon Lemon
Lemon trees were so prized in the Italian garden that they had their own special building – the *limonaia* – where they were cosseted through the winter. It is not certain when the lemon first arrived in Italy, but many kinds of citrus fruit were grown by the Romans, and by the 1550s there were more than 200 varieties at the Medici villa at Castello. They can live for many generations, given winter protection (with a minimum temperature of 9°C/48°F), regular feeding, occasional pruning, and careful watering: let the compost (soil mix) dry out almost completely, then give a thorough soak. *Citrus x mayeri* 'Meyer' is a handsome dwarf variety often bearing scented flowers and fruit in the same season. (See also page 141.)

Garden plan An Italianate town garden.

This plan draws on the symmetry, geometry and theatricality of the villa garden, playing with perceptions of distance to make the best use of a typically long, thin town garden. The space is divided into separate areas, making it feel much bigger. The curving hedge which sweeps right across the garden adds to the feeling of width; while cheating the proportions of the pool, so that it narrows towards the far end, makes it seem to extend further. The vista down the centre of the garden leads to a mirrored niche which reflects the water jet that is

the focal point of the pool, giving the illusion of further gardens and fountains beyond the hedge – this trickery is typical of the Italian garden. The illusion is emphasized by the cypresses rising above the hedge. Oversized urns and unexpected archways add to the drama, while behind the hedge are concealed two 'secret' areas, one hiding a working or play area, the other offering a shady secret retreat. Planting is confined to evergreen climbers and clipped shrubby planting, though roses might replace vines on the pergola. Seasonal colour could be introduced by planting up the urns.

There are many choices for the high hedge. Box and yew grow faster than is commonly supposed. Hornbeam is deciduous, but holds its autumn foliage well into the winter.

The pool is raised slightly from the surrounding gravel, and has a white stone edging.

Sheds, bins and a composting area can all be concealed behind the hedge.

A water jet is simple and lively, but a statue or urn would make an alternative focal point.

Parallel rows of topiary cones bring rhythm to the composition.

Gravel

Low-maintenance evergreen planting of aromatic shrubs. Large borders of acanthus could also be an option.

A pair of large urns flank the steps down into the garden.

A paved terrace is set at a higher level than the rest of the garden, and separated from it by a balustrade.

A central pergola planted with vines casts shade on either side as the sun moves round.

Planting list

1 Cypress (*Cupressus sempervirens*)

2 Topiary cones: choices include box (*Buxus sempervirens*), bay (*Laurus nobilis*) or yew (*Taxus baccata*)

3 Grape vine (*Vitis vinifera*)

4 Foxglove (*Digitalis purpurea*)

5 Plantain lily (*Hosta*)

6 Hedge: evergreens include box (*Buxus*) and yew (*Taxus*); hornbeam (*Carpinus*) is a deciduous option

7 Lemon (*Citrus limon*)

8 Evergreen planting such as curry plant (*Santolina*) or lavender.

Project **Training a box lolly**

A topiary lolly makes an attractive feature plant in the garden, and while it takes time to achieve, it is very satisfying to watch it take shape. You can make a successful lolly from any of the commonly used topiary plants, such as bay, euonymus or holly.

You will need

Topiary plant of your choice, such as *Buxus sempervirens* (box), *Ilex aquifolium* (holly), *Laurus nobilis* (bay tree) or something more unusual such as *Leptospermum*.

Pruning saw

Secateurs (pruners)

Supporting canes and twine for each plant

Foliar feed

Hand shears

Pots for the topiary balls – here lightweight fibreglass pots were used

Using box

• *Buxus sempervirens* is a classic choice for topiary because it is very hardy and its tight, compact foliage is ideal for shaping. However, its growth rate is very slow, so it will take a long time to establish.
• Box roots are dense and fibrous, so inserting the cane at step 3 may be a bit of a struggle. You will not hurt the plant, so just persevere.
• When deciding the height at stage 4, remember to allow for the height of the pot, if your lolly will be living in the ground.

1 To form a successful topiary lolly, it is important to select a plant with a strong, straight central stem. This shows a sturdy box. For a straight stem, you will need to start with a very young plant.

2 Cut away the extra stems with a pruning saw or secateurs, cutting downwards, flush with the stem, to keep it straight and smooth.

3 Insert a cane to the desired height of the lolly, then select your leader and tie it to the cane. Remove any unwanted large branches, but leave the thinner ones to feed the plant and fatten up the stalk.

4 Once the leader has reached the desired height, you can start forming the head. Cut away excess foliage at the top of the plant to reveal the head shape, but retain foliage below the head to keep it growing strongly until the head is fully formed.

5 Let the head develop, watering and feeding regularly with a foliar feed to encourage bushy growth, and trimming to keep the head growing into an even shape. Only when the head is fully formed should you cut away the basal growth.

6 The final stage is to trim the head into a perfectly manicured ball. The secret of shaping is to use very sharp hand shears or secateurs, and to view your topiary from all angles to make sure it does not become lop-sided.

The Islamic garden

Paradise, according to the Qur'an, is a garden: a garden of shady boughs and abundant fruit, palms and pomegranates, where the blessed recline on embroidered couches, cooled by fountains and tended by beauteous handmaidens. So when the first Arab Muslim armies swept into Persia in the 7th century and discovered gardens blooming in the desert, they could readily believe they had discovered heaven on earth. High walls shut out the cruel winds and sheltered fruit and fragrant blossom; planes and poplars cast deep pools of shade; tinkling rills and fountains refreshed the air. The invaders eagerly adopted these miraculous gardens as symbols of their faith, and for a thousand years, wherever Islam spread, the faithful created gardens in the Persian spirit, as havens of beauty and spiritual refreshment.

In an increasingly crowded and pressurized society, we have never had more need of gardens of this nature to give comfort, refuge and nourishment. The many water-saving techniques that Islamic gardens employ also provide ideas and inspiration as water becomes an increasingly precious resource.

Opposite
Le Jardin Majorelle in Marrakech, Morocco, was created in the 1920s as a calm, blue Art Deco version of the classic Islamic garden. It uses indigenous drought-resistant trees and plants as well as tough, exotic plants from all over the world, including bamboos from Indo-China and southern African lilies. Updated in the 1980s by fashion designers Yves St Laurent and Pierre Berge, there are now more than 300 plant species.

Above left and right
Just a few carefully chosen details will bring an Islamic flavour to the garden.

Gardens as visions of paradise

The high plateau of central Iran (formerly Persia) is a beautiful but harsh environment, ringed by mountain peaks and swept by fierce dust storms that blast across the plains. The winters are bitter, the summers scorching hot. Rainfall is minimal and, under the pitiless sun, the few rivers that enter the plateau soon peter out into dust and salt swamp. Yet, in these cruel conditions, the ancient Persians created gardens so beautiful that they came to embody the Islamic vision of paradise.

The conquering Muslims absorbed a garden tradition that was already over 1,000 years old. At Pasargadae, in modern Iran, you can still see the remains of the royal garden created by

Cyrus the Great in the 6th century BC – a rectangular space surrounded by colonnades and divided into four parts by intersecting limestone rills. It is the earliest known version of the *chahar bagh*, the symbolic fourfold layout that became the pattern for all Islamic gardens. Water, signifying the mercy of Allah, flows in four water-courses (representing the four rivers of life) that meet in a central pool or tank. At this point there may also be a viewing pavilion, reflected in the water: the garden is a place for spiritual contemplation, rather than work or play. Plants, too, have symbolic value: the cypress symbolizes mortality, the flowering almond regeneration.

Above left
The Taj Mahal in Agra, India, is a funerary garden created by Shah Jahan for his beloved wife Mumtaz Mahal. Beneath the main central arch an Arabic inscription reads "Only the pure in heart are invited to enter the Garden of Paradise".

Above right
In the Court of the Lions in the Alhambra Palace, four rivulets of water flow from small basins in the shady arcades that surround the courtyard, cooling and moistening the air.

Within 100 years of the death of the Prophet (in 632AD), Islam had established itself throughout the Middle East and spread to Egypt, North Africa and southern Spain. At a time when northern Europe had sunk into barbarism, Islamic scholars studied botany and medicine and collected plants from far and wide. In Spain, the Berbers (or Moors) established a garden tradition that still entrances us in the exquisite gardens of Granada, and which travelled in turn to Spanish America. In Persia, the caliphs continued to make gardens of fabulous beauty. Those descriptions in *The 1001 Nights* are not entirely fanciful – there really were gardens with trees of silver and gold, and hung with precious stones.

After seven centuries of sophisticated garden making, all was abruptly obliterated in the 13th century by the ravages of Genghis Khan. But even the Mongol hordes soon fell under the spell of the garden, and, within a generation, they too were making royal encampments with shady trees and silken tents. It was their descendants who established the Mughal Empire in India, creating during the 16th and 17th centuries, magnificent gardens around their palaces and tombs, culminating in the sublime beauty of the Taj Mahal.

No other garden form has had so long a life, or so widespread an influence. And in the 21st century, it seems to have more than ever to offer us. Its clean geometry, its use of simple, fine materials, its clever use of light and shade – these are key principles in the modern minimalist garden. The appreciation of water as a scarce resource, making a little go a long way, is a crucial lesson for today's garden makers. In an uncertain world, the serene symmetries of the Islamic garden speak of order and harmony. It offers us a physical and spiritual oasis, a place of refreshment and repose.

Below left
A water rill and sunken seating area in a modern garden take their cue from the Islamic tradition of clean lines and narrow channels of water.

Below right
Traditional Islamic architectural motifs, such as lacy stonework, can be combined with rich colours and resilient plants that thrive on heat and light and invoke elements of desert and jungle.

Precious water, cooling shade

To a desert people, no commodity is more valuable than water, and in the searing heat of the arid plain, no comfort could be greater than a pool of deep, cool shade. So these elements form the basis of the Islamic garden – a visual delight and a balm for all the senses.

The blessing of water

With no water to hand on the arid plateau, the ingenious Persians harnessed the snows of the surrounding peaks, carrying melt-water to their orchards and gardens through an elaborate system of underground tunnels or *qanats*, some up to 40km (25 miles) long. These emptied into tanks which fed, by force of gravity, the rills and fountains that adorned the gardens. Water channels were raised above the surrounding trees and flowerbeds, so that sluices could be opened to irrigate them.

Water is the very lifeblood of the Islamic garden, cooling the air and refreshing the senses in sparkling jets and bubbling fountains, small pools and rills. The rill is a supremely practical invention, distributing water to all parts of the garden, while keeping evaporation to a minimum; only a king could afford the profligacy of a wide mirror pool. By contrast, in 16th-century Kashmir, where water was plentiful, water moved in extravagant curtains down wide sloping screens or *chadars*, lit at night by candles concealed in niches: an effect copied in many modern urban spaces, such as the Parc André Citroën in Paris.

With recycling pumps allowing us to use water economically, Islamic-style water features have much to offer the modern garden. A reflecting pool, however small, offers tranquillity. A rill remains an elegant solution in a hot, sunny courtyard, and is safe where children play, while the rush of a water curtain is soothing and blocks out traffic noise in urban gardens.

Below left
In 18th-century European gardens, a 'Turkish Tent' was the height of fashion. This contemporary English garden has a modern version for shade.

Below right
A central raised pool, a key feature in the Islamic garden, is equally effective in a modern suburban setting.

Light and shade

Protection from the searing sun is essential in the Islamic garden, whether sitting in a deep, shady porch or open-sided pavilion or, perhaps, reclining beneath a silken canopy, as depicted in Mughal miniatures. While sari lengths make gorgeous temporary canopies, a more practical solution for the modern gardener may be a canvas sail stretched across a seating area, or perhaps a retractable awning fixed to the house. Inexpensive lightweight gazebos make excellent temporary pavilions, and are quick and easy to erect. More weighty versions, in rusted iron and sailcloth, make beautiful permanent additions to the garden, and are consistent with the Islamic appreciation of elaborate metalwork.

The stronger the sun, the sharper the shadow, and interplay of light and shadow is a major theme in the garden. Areas of cool darkness contrast with the bright reflective surfaces of water, stone and tile-work; natural plant shapes with geometric architectural forms.

A blank wall may be brought to life by arranging plants to cast interesting shadows, a trick borrowed by many urban gardeners. Bamboo and palms deliver a particularly graphic effect. Pierced screens and lanterns also create beautiful shadow-play on walls and pavements, often made even richer by the addition of stained glass.

Above right
The dramatic use of shadows adds an extra dimension of interest in this Marrakech courtyard.

Above left
Elaborate ironwork screens are here developed into a fanciful gazebo.

Tutorial Making every drop of water count

Water represented the mercy of Allah, so it was regarded as a sin to waste it. The Islamic garden-makers were masters of water conservation, devising ingenious methods of saving this most precious of natural resources and using it to maximum effect in the garden. The seven water-saving steps that follow will help you to use water just as efficiently in your own garden.

Harvest your rainwater

A surprisingly large amount of water can be collected from the roof of a house, or even a shed, and easily diverted into storage tanks rather than disappearing down the drain. Even the run-off from a drive or patio can be successfully harvested. In a smaller garden, look out for one of the many new decorative styles of water-butt, that can be positioned by a down-pipe and integrated into the garden rather than hidden away. Where more space is available, substantial plastic oil tanks may be hidden round the side of the house, concealed behind trellis or beneath decking, or even cunningly disguised as a garden folly. Tanks fill up quickly when it rains, so feed any overflows or down-pipes to ponds or other water features.

Make use of greywater

If every time you run the hot water tap, empty your water glass or drain your pasta, you collect the waste water into a jug or bowl, you will find you can fill up several watering cans each day. Water from showers and baths is also well worth saving: the most efficient way is to plumb the waste pipes directly into a tank or water-butt, but, if this is not possible, you can empty the bath quite quickly and efficiently by means of a siphon pump attached to a hose, which you can feed into a butt or directly on to your garden. Use mild vegetable soaps and shampoos, and do not pour greywater directly on to plants, but on the soil around them. Do not use water that is very greasy, or that contains bleach or strong detergents.

Conserve soil moisture

Digging in lots of organic matter can radically improve the water-holding capacity of your soil, allowing rain to penetrate more deeply, and more water to be absorbed. A thick mulch applied in the spring, when the soil is at its wettest, will help to keep that moisture trapped in the soil. Well-rotted garden compost, stable manure, chipped bark or mushroom compost all make excellent mulches, and will rot down to improve the structure of your soil as well as reducing water loss. Sheet mulches are also effective, and you will also save hours of weeding by planting through plastic or geotextile membranes. Wet newspapers covered with grass clippings or compost make for a cheap eco-friendly alternative.

Water without waste

A seep-hose system, with porous tubing buried beneath a thick layer of mulch, is an efficient option for beds and borders, while an automatic drip irrigation system is the best way to deal with a large number of pots. For precise targeting, use the good old watering can. An old-fashioned but effective technique is to make a shallow depression round a plant, building up the surrounding soil into a little wall. When you water into this moat, the water remains concentrated over the roots, where it is needed most. To get water right down to the roots of a tree or shrub, sink a pipe or inverted bottle into the ground to the side of the roots. A flowerpot sunk by each plant will do a similar job in the greenhouse – a good idea for tomatoes, which need copious and regular watering.

Choose water-wise planting

With water supplies becoming increasingly unpredictable, it makes sense to grow plants that can cope with less water. There are many ideas for drought-tolerant planting in other chapters. Those shown here are *Sedum* 'Matrona' (right) and *Allium* 'Purple Sensation' (far right).

Water at the right time

Early in the morning or late in the evening are the best times to water, when evaporation rates are low and water has a chance to soak into the soil. If you don't fancy an early start, most garden centres sell watering systems that work on an automated timer. You will get the best value by setting it to work at night, when water pressure will be at its highest and evaporation levels at their lowest. A thorough soak, at longer intervals, is better for your plants than watering little and often.

Water selectively

Concentrate your efforts on containers, seedlings and anything that is newly planted, being careful to water the soil rather than the leaves. Your next priorities should be fruit and vegetables when the fruits, tubers or pods are swelling. Young trees can be thirsty, especially early in the summer, and will need generous watering for the first two years, as will new hedges if they are to establish quickly. Do not bother with turf unless it is recently seeded or laid: a parched lawn soon recovers.

A love of plants

To the Muslim, every perfect flower is a reminder of the spirit of God at work in creation. So beautiful plants, in all their variety of form and fragrance, are essential in the modern paradise garden.

Islam teaches reverence for nature, and, over the centuries, many European travellers commented on the Islamic love of flowers. A Moorish gardening treatise of the early 12th century speaks of jasmine trailing over trellis, aromatic herbs and roses, two exciting new fruits – the lemon and the medlar – and familiar ornamentals such as lavender and oleander, hollyhocks and hibiscus, colocasias, poppies and iris.

Oriental planes and poplars have been grown from the earliest times for their dense shade along with almonds, plums, apricots and quinces, apples and pears: the Islamic paradise promises two of every kind of fruit. In subtropical regions, date palms often take the place of planes: the beautiful Garden of the Golden Book, created for a palace in Abu Dhabi, has evergreen planting based on 12 towering date palms. The modern town garden closely resembles the enclosed *chahar bagh*, and many modern fruit varieties are ideal for small gardens, especially if trained into decorative fans or cordons.

Many of the native plants of these arid regions are familiar spring bulbs, including tulips, hyacinths, crocus and narcissus, plants that are able to complete their life-cycles before the searing heat of summer. The gardens would have been superb in spring, with jewel-bright bulbs beneath sheets of blossom. Pathways ran alongside the water channels, raised above the level of the flowerbeds, so that walking across the garden would seem like walking over a carpet of flowers. Real carpets were laid down on lawns of clover – much more durable than grass.

Today, the *chahar bagh* design (see pages 26, 35) can be adapted to many styles of planting. A modern urban courtyard, for example, might use no more than a few spears of iris and a stand of bamboo, while at La Mortella in Ischia, Italy, a sequence of Islamic-style pools and rills are surrounded by a lush tropical planting of bright colours and giant foliage. To create a paradise garden, it clearly makes sense to choose the plants you most enjoy.

Below
The Hamilton Botanic Gardens in New Zealand have a modern recreation of the Islamic garden with typical carpet-style planting.

Plant focus Plants of paradise

In the oasis of the Islamic garden, fruit trees and colourful flowers provide a feast for the senses, beguiling to the eye, exquisite in fragrance and delicious to eat.

Prunus dulcis Almond tree

The almond has been cultivated for over 5,000 years, and has a special place in the Islamic garden, both for its beautiful spreading branches and its pink-white blossom, with its symbolic promise of new life in spring. The common almond closely resembles its close relatives, the peach and cherry, but has a much stronger fragrance. 'Macrocarpa' is one of the best edible varieties. Remember you will need two trees: almonds must cross-pollinate to produce flowers and nuts. (See also page 144.)

Prunus dulcis 'Macrocarpa'   *Punica granatum*

Punica granatum Pomegranate

Pomegranate is singled out as one of the heavenly fruits and the Prophet Mohammed decreed that his followers should eat pomegranates "to purge the body of longing". In other cultures, however, it is associated with fertility, and is given as a wedding gift. Pomegranates make striking pot plants with their shiny, dark green foliage and vivid red blossoms, but beware their sharp thorns. (See also page 145.)

Papaver somniferum Opium poppy

The narcotic and sleep-inducing properties of the opium poppy were well known to Islamic herbalists. It often appears in miniatures and even features in the decoration of the Taj Mahal. The Persians grew a simple single form, but today there are many more eye-catching varieties, with elaborate ruffled blooms, ranging from pink and scarlet to purple and black.

Rosa damascena

Rosa Rose

Legend has it that the rose was created from a drop of perspiration that fell from the Prophet Mohammed's brow, so the rose has pride of place in the Islamic garden. Red roses, probably the damask rose *Rosa damascena*, have been grown for centuries in Persia to make attar of roses, the most highly prized of scents and flavourings. They are also a major theme in Persian poetry, so choose *R.* 'Omar Khayam', named after the most famous of Persian poets and the author of the *Rubaiyat*, along with the Persian yellow rose *R. foetida* 'Persiana' and the gorgeously fragrant *R.* x *damascena* var. *semperflorens*. (See also page 146.)

Papaver somniferum hybrid

Decorative elements

Islamic gardens are often highly decorated, with colourful tiles and mosaic-work, and elaborate architectural details such as wrought-iron lanterns, or wood or marble panels worked into astonishingly light and lacy-looking designs.

Right
This Essex garden has a central raised pool and simple block seating, both covered with Islamic-style tiles and panels of mosaic. These details are offset against regular paving squares.

Below
The influence of the Islamic garden can be clearly seen in this modern town garden, created by Helen Dillon. A broad rill is set in simple white limestone, with decoration supplied by deep banks of intricate planting.

Early Islam forbade the depiction of living forms, but the sensuous arabesques and complex twining patterns that reappear in the gardens strongly suggest the natural forms of flowers, twigs and vines. In later centuries, Persian and Mughal artists painted life-like representations of gardens in miniature, while floral motifs were common in Mughal gardens. The white marble walls of the Taj Mahal sparkle with flowers, inlaid in semi-precious stones. In modern gardens, flowerheads or petals are often floated on water, scattered like confetti.

Just a suggestion of these decorative forms can be enough to bring an Islamic flavour to the garden – a glazed rill, a Moroccan lantern or even

a simple tile set into the wall. The garden above, for example, has a typical raised pool as a centre-piece, while panels of mosaic-work and deep blue tiles reappear throughout the garden. The colour was suggested by the vivid blue walls of the Majorelle Garden in Marrakech. In Islam, as in Christianity, blue is the colour of heaven.

The demanding water requirements of a green lawn means that different design options should be considered. One option is to replace a lawn with drought-tolerant plants. Another approach, used in a Dublin garden (see left), is to introduce a canal in place of the lawn. Such a feature need not waste water; it can be shallow, it can use recycled water, and be topped up by rainwater. Leaving aside the benefits of sustainability and ease of maintenance, the simplicity, purity and balance of this scheme sums up the essence of the Islamic garden – a sense of spaciousness and quiet, of separation from the everyday world. It is a superb example of how Islamic ideas can transform a small town garden in a busy suburb into a private paradise.

Garden plan A contemporary chahar bagh

Four is a sacred number in Islam. There are four walled gardens in Paradise planted with four fruits – fig, pomegranate, olive and date – and refreshed by four fountains, with water channels representing the four rivers of life – milk, honey, water and wine.

This plan for a small walled garden is based on the number four and follows the traditional Islamic *chahar bagh* plan of watercourses intersecting at right angles. A pair of jasmine-draped arbours and an open-sided pavilion provide shady places to sit. Instead of the traditional oriental plane or white poplar, too large for a small garden, the pavilion is flanked by flowering almonds. The walls are clothed with fruit and blossom: peaches, nectarines, apricots and figs trained on the sunny walls; morello cherries and roses on the shadier ones. Each of the four beds is dominated by a central cypress, rising above low plantings of spring bulbs and ground-cover roses. Palms and pomegranates grow in pots, which can be moved indoors for the winter.

Planting list

1 Flowering almond (*Prunus dulcis* 'Macrocarpa')

2 Peach (*Prunus persica*)

3 Nectarine (*Prunus persica* var. *nectarina*)

4 Apricot (*Prunus armenica*)

5 Fig (*Ficus carica*)

6 Morello cherry (*Prunus cerasus*)

7 *Rosa* 'New Dawn'

8 Cypress (*Cupressus sempervirens*)

9 Fan palm (*Chamaerops humilis*)

10 Cyclamen (*Cyclamen hederifolium*)

11 Crocus (*Crocus tommasinianus*)

12 Lily-of-the-valley (*Convallaria majalis*)

13 Lady's mantle (*Alchemilla mollis*)

14 Pomegranate (*Punica granatum*)

15 Sun-loving spring bulbs and ground-cover roses

Many climbing roses such as *Rosa* 'New Dawn' grow happily on shadier walls.

Slender evergreen cypress provides year-long structure.

The pale spring blossom of the almond tree is deliciously fragrant.

Pavilion

Arbour

Shady wall

The almond tree is underplanted with a combination of cyclamen, crocus and lily-of-the-valley, and shade-tolerant *Alchemilla mollis*.

The rills are lined with turquoise ceramic tiles, which contrast with the simple white limestone paving.

Fountain jets

While the date palm is characteristic of subtropical Islamic gardens, the fan palm is more in scale with a smaller garden.

The sunny wall (not shown) would be planted with fan-trained peach, nectarine and apricot trees, which offer delightful blossom in spring.

Limestone paving

Project Constructing a simple rill

A rill makes a wonderful addition to a garden, either enclosed with hedges as a self-contained feature or as a centrepiece for a formal layout. The narrow channel allows water to animate a long stretch of garden, losing little water to evaporation.

You will need

Peg and line

Marker paint

Spade

Concrete mix for base

Breeze (cinder) blocks and/or brick for the retaining walls

Mortar

Spirit level

Pond underlay

Butyl liner

Heavy blocks, for weights

3 bridge pavers – the ones used here are 50cm x 1m (2 x 3ft)

Square concrete setts for edging the rill, in a contrasting colour to the bridge pavers. The number of these can be calculated according to the length and area of your rill design.

Soil for backfilling

Plain gravel

Rill materials

• The materials chosen are inexpensive and widely available: concrete paving slabs and setts and plain gravel.
• Polished limestone paving and planters could be substituted for a sharper, modern look.

1 Make a drawing of your rill design so you can estimate quantities of materials. Mark out the rill, using a peg and line and marker paint to inscribe a perfect circle.

2 The block retaining wall should have a width of 30–60cm (12–24in) and a depth of 25–45cm (10–18in), depending on the block's size. The concrete foundation must be at least 10cm (4in) deep, so allow for this when digging out the rill.

3 Line your rill with concrete, being sure to make a level base, and use breeze blocks to build the retaining walls.

4 Test every block to make sure it is level. When the mortar has set, line the base with a layer of pond underlay or old carpet, then place the liner on top, pushing it into the corners of the rill and folding it neatly. Hold the edges in place with heavy blocks.

5 Start filling the rill with water. The addition of water will stretch the liner, allowing you to fine-tune the folds as it fills. Lay the bridge pavers firmly into position.

6 Dress the edge of the rill with a row of contrasting setts. Trim the liner just beyond the edging stones. There is no need to dress the base of the rill. Tuck any excess liner down the side of the wall, backfill with soil and finish off with gravel.

The patio garden

In the ancient Moorish cities and sun-baked whitewashed villages of Andalucía, the great Islamic garden tradition evolved into a uniquely Spanish style – the patio garden designed to offer seclusion, peace and shelter from the blistering sun.

The patio is not just a garden, it is a sanctuary. A room of four high walls, open to the sky, indivisible from the building that surrounds it. It might be a simple yard, glimpsed through a curlicue of wrought-iron grillework, with a handful of scarlet geraniums in a can. It may be festooned with flowers and fragrant herbs, with a tumble of bougainvillea cascading down the walls. Or a place of austerity, with just a twisted fig tree or a dusty oil jar for decoration.

A confined space with little or no soil may not seem ideal conditions for a garden. But the enclosure designed to offer coolness and shade to people, also offers particular benefits for plants, especially in colder latitudes. The shelter, warmth and intimacy of the patio offers the opportunity to experiment with plants that would not thrive in the open garden, and to combine them in new and creative ways.

Opposite
In the Spanish city of Córdoba, lack of space is no hindrance to creative gardening. Their patios overflow with architectural features, pots, bright colours and wall-mounted decorations.

Above left
In a small space, you can really appreciate decorative details, such as this Islamic-style tiling.

Above right
Geraniums in wall-hung pots probably evoke the Mediterranean more than any other plant. Here, an attractive wrought-iron wall structure supports the pots and the white wall creates a sun-drenched silhouette.

Andalucía and Mexico: patios in the sun

Contemporary patio gardens have their roots in two quite different styles – the plantaholic profusion of Andalucía, and the spare architectural minimalism developed by the great designer Luis Barragán in Mexico. But, interestingly, the second style derives directly from the first. Both are responses to living in the heat of the city – and their qualities of coolness and repose have much to offer modern urban dwellers in a warming climate.

The patio gardens of southern Spain are the legacy of 700 years of Moorish rule: enclosed oases of coolness and colour to give shelter from the sweltering sun. The most famous of these are the patios of the Alhambra Palace at Granada, built in the 13th and 14th centuries: sublime compositions of lacy stonework and reflecting water, shadow and light. At nearby Córdoba, the heart of the Great

Mosque is a patio believed to be the oldest garden in Europe. More intimate in scale are the private courtyard gardens that adorn every corner of the city. In late spring, for a brief and brilliant fortnight, the heavy street doors are thrown open and these secret gardens are shared in the annual Festival of the Patios. Balconies groan with blossom; every inch of wall is crammed with pots and planters; tomatoes and aubergines ripen sweetly in the sun; while shady corners are full of ferns and dozing cats. Traditional Islamic decoration – elaborate ironwork, sparkling fountains and jewel-coloured tiles – is overlaid with exuberant Mediterranean planting, and anything and everything is pressed into service as a pot. For these are gardens composed almost entirely of containers, providing vibrant and colourful inspiration for every urban gardener.

Above
The extravagant colours and decorations of the Spanish-style patio cover every inch of wall and floor.

The concept of the enclosed patio garden travelled with the conquistadors to the Americas, where they found even greater need for coolness and refreshment. But, building their houses from adobe, the smooth, fat garden walls became less of a backdrop and more of a feature in their own right, and Mediterranean white and blue was exchanged for vibrant earth colours. In the mid-20th century, Mexican designer Luis Barragán distilled this homely rustic style to make an entirely new kind of patio garden: one with every inessential pared away until each element in the garden – steps, or pots, or growing plants – became a piece of pure sculpture. Amid the thronging tumult of Mexico City, Barragán created spaces of a luminous stillness, designed (as was the Islamic garden) to nurture the sprit. "My house is my refuge," he wrote, "and the garden is the soul of the house." No wonder these calm, uncluttered gardens still appeal so strongly to stressed-out city dwellers today, inspiring a new generation of architects and garden-makers to experiment with strongly architectural gardens in which plants play a secondary role to the drama of the 'outdoor room'.

Barragán's hallmarks are easy enough to copy, but curiously hard to get right. They include walls rendered in glowing colours, minimalist rills and chutes of water, and crisp cubes of space enlivened by simple sculptural ornament, whether the silhouette of a shapely tree or a carefully arranged group of pots. In this pure language, quality of materials is all. Whereas in the Andalucían patio, any jolly, colourful improvisation will do, the minimalist patio requires beautifully finished walls, finely executed stonework, and plants which are few but of supremely elegant form.

For many gardeners who enjoy simple, modern interiors, a Barragán-style patio offers a harmonious extension of their indoor space. Successful minimalism is neither cold nor sterile, but offers a strong, calm, uncluttered space to refresh the mind and spirit.

Below
The Hacienda Santa Rosa in Valle de Bravo, Mexico, designed by Jose de Yturbe, demonstrates the minimalist vocabulary of the modern Mexican style. Yet the warm yellow suffuses it with warmth, while the design embraces the elements, with pools of sunshine, dramatic shadows, and the welcome presence of the natural world beyond the walls.

Creating a sense of seclusion

Within the confines of the patio garden, you can create whatever mood you choose – whether minimalist purity or a fiesta of exuberant profusion. Your choice of materials and plants will all contribute to the atmosphere, as will sound, shade and lighting.

Opposite
This terracotta wall sets the mood, and the canvas canopy gives welcome shade.

Below left
Pink washed walls give warmth to this pebbled courtyard and a strong background for the containers of citrus trees and box.

Below right
Architectural detail, ornament and planting provide maximum interest in this patio.

Wonder walls

If you are lucky enough to have walls of mellow stone or lovely, old, moss-aged brick, do no more than sit back and admire them. Most of us, however, will need to work harder to make our walls or fences into a fitting backdrop for the garden. The typical sun-drenched patio look is achieved through the use of coloured renders (the big advantage of renders, as opposed to paint, is that they require no maintenance). Unless your climate is excessively hot, when a white surface helps to deflect the heat, pure white can be difficult to live with – it looks cold and dismal in winter, and glaringly bright in summer. The bold ochres, pinks and terracottas favoured by many Mexican designers make a dramatic statement, but remember that these need strong light and blue skies to be shown to advantage, and will look crudely overpowering in watery northern light. It is preferable to use soft earthy pinks and sand colours in such regions.

Almost any wall or fence, however ugly, can be successfully disguised with a dressing of plants. Even a shady wall will support a range of lovely climbers, including glossy-leaved ivies (*Hedera*), curtains of *Clematis alpina*, the beautiful lace-cap *Hydrangea petiolaris* or even finer *Schizophragma hydrangeoides*, as well as shade-tolerant roses such as *Rosa* 'Madame Alfred Carrière', *R.* 'New Dawn' or climbing *R.* 'Teasing Georgia', a New English yellow rose with a gorgeous guava-like scent. Fragrance really comes into its own in the patio garden, trapped by the high warm walls. So, make room for honeysuckles, early-flowering *Clematis armandii* or chocolate-scented *Akebia quinata*, which also have the benefit of being evergreen.

On a sunny, sheltered wall, you are spoilt for choice. Wisterias will flower profusely in this position, but need plenty of room. The passion flowers are long-lasting, easy and evergreen. *Passiflora caerulea* is the hardiest and most widely grown or opt for dayglo-pink *P.* x *exoniensis*, which looks wildly exotic, but is hardy to -5°C (23°F). Alternatively, choose a wall shrub such as pineapple-scented *Cytisus battandieri* or joyous yellow *Fremontodendron californicum* 'California Glory', which will bask in this choice position.

Fabulous floors

The intricate pebble mosaics in many Spanish and Italian gardens show how the choice of a floor can rise above the utilitarian to offer a whole new area of creativity to the garden. As well as stone, brick, pebble and tile, hard surfaces may be made of wood, such as decking, which always has an air of the seaside; or railway sleepers, which give a rugged, rustic

look. Metal gridwork or glass tiles have quite the opposite effect – sleek and urban. Concrete is an endlessly versatile material, that can be fashioned into imitation stonework, or poured, coloured, shaped and polished into a variety of finishes. Or where safety is important, recycled rubber is an excellent choice, and can introduce an element of bold colour to the garden.

Above
A simple geometric pattern in pebbles makes a beautiful floor for any patio garden.

Left
Terracotta tiles are a traditional choice in the Mediterranean, here enlivened with ceramic insets.

Tutorial | Planting into paving

A paved patio offers the opportunity to grow a few plants directly in the ground. Choose plants that do not mind being trodden on and that would naturally thrive in harsh, stony conditions with little soil round the roots. Mediterranean plants such as thyme (*Thymus*) and common sage (*Salvia officinalis*) are very suitable, and release their fragrance when people brush past them. Regular pickings for the kitchen will stop the sage getting woody.

1 Use a hammer and chisel to break up the mortar all round the paving stone. Scrape out the debris using the chisel until the stone is free.

2 Use a crowbar to lift the stone, and remove it. Break up the concrete and hardcore in the planting hole, removing the largest pieces.

3 Mix some loam-based potting mix with a handful or two of horticultural grit. Plant, firm in and water well. Top-dress with a mulch of gravel.

Soothing sounds

The sound of running water is a real asset to a patio garden. This can be achieved in the smallest of spaces by installing recirculating water features such as a cast-iron wall fountain, a lion-head spouting into a stone basin, or a minimalist letterbox chute emptying into a rill or grille. Ensure that the flow of the water is carefully adjusted to a musical trickle. To save water, choose water features that pump water from an integrated reservoir. In prolonged hot weather, these will need topping up – a good use for grey water providing it is clean, and will not clog pumps and filters. The sound of water is not only soothing, but also remarkably effective at screening out traffic noise and the other unwelcome sounds of the city. So, too, is the rustle of bamboo or the gentle tinkle of wind chimes. Some city gardeners even introduce recorded birdsong. In the sheltered environment of the patio, such sounds will not become over-insistent and will add to the atmosphere of the garden.

Creating shade

While Spanish-style buildings usually have a covered colonnade or veranda, most of us will have to construct a shaded area. A simple wooden framework can support climbing plants on wires or a removable canvas canopy. Wind-out awnings are convenient, but can be expensive. In reality, as most patio gardens are small, with surrounding walls casting shadow during different parts of the day, you may find an easily moveable shade, in the form of a large parasol, is a better solution.

Summer nights

Just as a shady patio is a refuge in the heat of the day, it can become a magical outdoor room in the cool of the evening. The key is atmospheric lighting – not too bright, but warm and subtle, picking out particular features such as a fine group of pots or a handsome plant. For the best effect, conceal the source of the light and direct it from the side or from below. This will give the subject more depth and texture than lighting it from the front.
A pleasing effect in a small space is to wash a wall in light, creating a softly glowing backdrop to show off plant or other silhouettes: this works particularly well on plain rendered walls. For permanent lighting, it is well worth consulting a specialist company, but do not forget what enchanting effects you can achieve by using simple features like fairy lights, lanterns and flares.

Tutorial **Pots of inspiration**

There are few things that can't be grown successfully in containers, from exotic trees and colourful flowers, to delicious fresh vegetables and herbs. In fact, pots have many advantages – they are easy to maintain; they can be moved around according to mood and season; and each plant can be given its preferred conditions.

Choose your style

Containers are an easy and direct way to create a garden style, and by massing them together you can make full use of every inch of space – and enjoy tremendous plant combinations that you could never achieve in open ground. Limiting yourself to just one or two materials or colours will prevent a small space looking too cluttered.

It is no accident that terracotta remains the most popular choice: it is adaptable to many garden styles and sets off nearly every plant to advantage. It is, however, heavy to handle, easy to break, susceptible to frost damage, and extremely porous. There are many excellent plastic imitations that avoid these pitfalls, although, of course, they will never age as gracefully as real terracotta. If such cheating is unthinkable, line your clay pot with plastic to inhibit water loss.

Glazed ceramics and resin containers lose less water and are available in a huge range of colours. Wooden half barrels give a rustic look and wooden Versailles planters a supremely sophisticated one. Both will need regular coats of wood preservative or paint. Reconstituted stone is now available in both classical and modern designs, and, being very heavy, is ideal for top-heavy shrubs or trees. For an edgy modern look, consider metals or glass (though these will both get hot in direct sunshine.) Alternatively, recycle the contents of kitchen or shed for a heart-warming, eclectic jumble.

Below left
Do not neglect walls and fences as suitable homes for containers. But small pots like these will need more frequent watering.

Below centre
Warm and versatile, terracotta remains the most traditional choice for the garden.

Below right
For a more modern, minimalist look, repeat strong geometric shapes in a metallic finish.

Compost for pots

For seasonal displays such as summer bedding, any good-quality, peat-free multi-purpose potting mix will do. For permanent plantings, a loam-based potting mix such as John Innes no 3 is much better. (John Innes is not a brand of potting mix, but a series of different sterile soil-based formulations devised for different stages of plant growth.) Loam-based potting mixes hold their nutrients for longer, dry out less readily and, when dry, are considerably easier to re-wet. Also, being heavier, they help to keep larger pots steady. Plants that cannot tolerate lime, such as camellias, azaleas and acers, will need an ericaceous (lime-free) potting mix. Water-retaining gels and controlled release fertilizers can be added to the pot before planting. (Remember to wet your water-retaining granules before you add

Right
An automatic watering system, with a probe measuring the moisture levels in each pot, is the most efficient and economical way to keep large numbers of pots watered.

Below
The sheltered microclimate of the patio offers ideal conditions to grow plants, such as *Echeveria*, which are borderline tender.

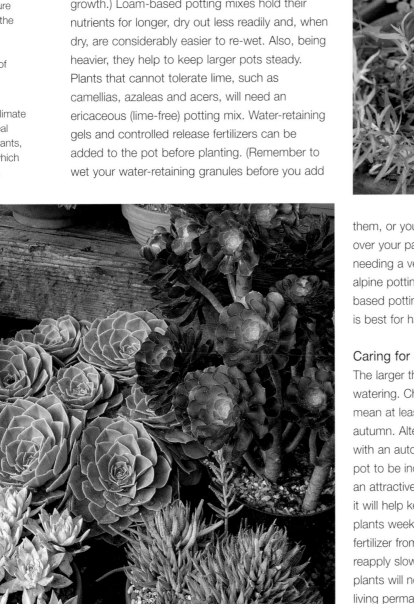

them, or your pot will erupt and spew jelly all over your patio!) For alpines and succulents needing a very sharp drainage, use a proprietary alpine potting mix or add grit to a suitable loam-based potting mix. A soil-less mix, being lighter, is best for hanging baskets.

Caring for containers

The larger the pot, the less often it will need watering. Check moisture regularly – that will mean at least once a day from mid-spring to early autumn. Alternatively, choose a micro-irrigation kit with an automatic controller, which will allow each pot to be individually watered. Either way, choose an attractive mulch for the surface of your pot – it will help keep weeds out and moisture in. Feed plants weekly with a general-purpose liquid fertilizer from four to six weeks after planting, or reapply slow-release fertilizer as directed. Some plants will need regular dead-heading. Plants living permanently in containers will need repotting every two to five years. In between, perk them up at the beginning of the growing season by scraping away as much as you can of the old potting mix – aim for 3–5cm (1¼–2in) – and replacing it with a fresh layer.

Garden plans Pots for the patio garden

Container arrangement for a sunny corner

The sheltered microclimate of the patio offers the ideal opportunity to grow plants that are borderline tender. This combination of pots for a sunny area of patio has a core planting of three fine foliage plants, offering both fragrance and variety of form and texture.

Plant list

1 Japanese mock orange (*Pittosporum tobira*)

2 Honey bush (*Melianthus major*)

3 Honey spurge (*Euphorbia mellifera*)

4 French lavender (*Lavandula stoechas*)

5 Silverbush (*Convolvulus cneorum*)

6 *Osteospermum* 'Whirligig'

7 Madonna lily (*Lilium longiflorum*)

The *Pittosporum* can be left to grow into a small shapely tree or clipped into a ball or dome.

Melianthus has large, deeply serrated leaves in bright silver and spectacular red flowers.

Right at the front (4, 5 and 6) are three easy-to-grow, drought-tolerant plants that will flower all summer long: the French lavender, silver-leaved *Convolvulus cneorum* and osteospermums.

These strongly scented lilies will not last long, but will be glorious while they do. They can be replaced when their moment is over by later-flowering bulbs such as *Galtonia candicans* or agapanthus.

Container arrangement for a shady corner

A patio garden, surrounded by walls, will always have an area that spends much of the time in shade. Here is a chance to grow plants with elegant, glossy foliage and cool white or pale lime blooms that glimmer in the shadows.

Strongly architectural *Fatsia japonica* will thrive in shady conditions.

While *Hydrangea arborescens* 'Annabelle' is deciduous, it has a long season of interest, the white blooms fading to lime, then drying neatly on the plant to last through the winter.

In winter, replace the tobacco plants and hosta with hellebores and a bowl of snowdrops, and enjoy the crisp silhouette of a sphere of box.

Plant list

1 False castor oil plant (*Fatsia japonica*)

2 Hart's tongue fern (*Asplenium scolopendrium*)

3 Camellia (*Camellia japonica*)

4 *Hydrangea arborescens* 'Annabelle'

5 Tobacco plant (*Nicotiana alata* 'Lime Green')

6 *Hosta* 'Frances Williams'

7 Box (*Buxus sempervirens*)

Plant focus Sizzling colour

With their long-lasting vibrant colours, easy-going ways and love of sunshine, no other plants evoke so completely the riotous sun-drenched patios of southern Spain as *Bougainvillea* and *Pelargonium*. (See also pages 141–2.)

Bougainvillea

No climber offers better value, flowering for months at a time in scorching shades of magenta, purple, orange and scarlet. In a frost-free setting 'boogies' can stay outside all year round, but, in cooler climes, treat them like pelargoniums or fuchsias, cutting them back hard and bringing them indoors for the winter. Bougainvilleas are evergreen in warm climates, but drop their leaves when the temperature falls below 10°C (50°F). Given a little heat, however, they will continue flowering, blooming through the winter on leafless stems. They are vigorous, not to say rampant, and will tend to surge upwards, so train them firmly along horizontal wires if you wish to cover a wall. They will look equally good scrambling over a pergola or cascading from wall-mounted containers. There are well over 100 varieties to choose from, including dwarf, variegated and double forms. Popular varieties include *B.* 'Scarlett O'Hara' and *B.* x *buttiana* 'Mrs Butt'.

Pelargonium Geranium

The species *Pelargonium*, known to many as the geranium, is a half-hardy shrub from South Africa. It was brought to Europe in the 17th century by sailing ships from the Dutch East India Company, and has remained a firm favourite ever since, There are countless cultivars, but they can be roughly divided into four main groups:

Bougainvillea glabra

Pelargonium graveolens 'Little Gem' (scented)

Drought-resistant zonal pelargoniums.

1 Zonal pelargoniums are the largest group, with rounded leaves marked with a distinct dark zone, and single or double flowers. There is a whole sub-group of dwarf forms, which are ideal for containers.

2 Regal pelargoniums are rather more delicate than the indestructible zonals. They have deeply serrated leaves and wide, trumpet-shaped flowers in all kinds of exotic colours, including black and white. They are some of the earliest to flower.

3 Ivy-leaved pelargoniums are so called because they have the lobed leaves and characteristic trailing form of ivy. The leaves are generally glossy and the trailing habit can extend anywhere from 15cm–2m (6in–6½ft), making them spectacular in wall containers or hanging baskets.

4 Scented-leaved pelargoniums are grown mainly for their attractive, strongly perfumed leaves. Although the five-petalled flowers are smaller than most of the other hybrids and the flowering season shorter, the blooms are borne in profusion, which adds to their charm.

Other sub-groups include pansy-flowered Angels, Rosebud, Cactus and the deceptively delicate-looking Stellar pelargoniums, their names reflecting the appearance of the flowers. All enjoy a sunny spot and grow happily in tubs, window boxes and hanging baskets. Fed regularly with a high-potash feed, they will flower from spring right through to late autumn. Protect them from frost during the winter months and they will continue to thrive for many years.

Pelargonium 'Lord Bute' *is one of the showiest of regal pelargoniums.*

Pelargonium 'Toscana Erke' (ivy-leaved)

Project Creating a hanging herb garden

In this project, old tins have been recycled into colourful containers planted with an assortment of herbs. The tins can be hung on a wall or from a windowsill – or anywhere you please. It's a great way of making use of vertical space in the patio.

You will need

Hammer

Large nail

Tin cans

Medium grade sandpaper

Masking tape

Enamel spray paint

Twine

Lightweight polystyrene (Styrofoam) for filling the pot bases

Herbs of your choice such as coriander (cilantro), parsley, thyme, sage, mint, rosemary and lemon balm.

Cup-hooks

Herb pot tips

• When piercing drainage holes in the tin base, place the tin on a damp cloth to stop it from slipping.
• Use tarred twine to hang the pots – it looks good and is slow to rot.
• Wipe over the pots with WD40 before the winter to stop them going rusty. Do not spray it on, or you may get it on the herbs.

1 Using a hammer and a large nail, bash drainage holes in the base of the tin. You will also need to make three hanging holes in the sides of the tins (they will hang more steadily with three holes rather than two).

2 Sand down the surface of the tins with a medium grade sandpaper, so that the paint keys properly. Don't forget the base, which will be visible when hanging.

3 The tins are to be decorated with bands of two colours. Use masking tape to create straight lines and prevent spray drifting on to the bands you have already painted. Remember to remove the tape promptly.

4 Spray the tins with enamel spray paint, which is quick and easy to use. Choose a selection of bright and cheerful colours to set off the greens of the herbs.

5 Thread the tins with long, double-lengths of twine for hanging and, rather than filling the base with crocks, use small pieces of lightweight polystyrene to make them lighter and easier to hang.

6 Plant up the tins with your favourite herbs – a mixture of herbs in each tin looks best – and suspend them from cup-hooks along the length of the windowsill. Do not hang them all at the same height, as a relaxed jumble looks most effective.

The Mediterranean garden

It is in the sun-drenched lands of the Mediterranean that gardening began, with sacred groves and mountain-tops, with wheat and vines and figs and olives. For today's water-starved gardener, there is no richer source of inspiration. The rocky hillsides of wind-sculpted pines and silvery olives offer a magical lexicon of beautiful, fragrant, drought-resistant plants that will thrive with the bare minimum of attention. Yet the same climate nurtures the great plant collections of the Riviera, among the proudest achievements of the garden-maker's art, almost overwhelming in their luxuriance. Everywhere there is fragrance – the resinous tang of cypress and pine, sweet notes of lavender, bitter artemisia, pungent rosemary, the dusty aroma of sage. Everywhere there is colour: cobalt skies and turquoise seas, the red-tiled roofs and painted shutters of the village houses, fields of sunflowers and lavender, the unearthly glow of yellow spring blossom lighting up the trees at dawn. The Mediterranean garden is a feast for all the senses. But it is also, in a changing climate, a responsible and intelligent way to garden.

Opposite
Yellow spring blossom and colourful succulents light up the Mediterranean garden.

Above left
A Mediterranean-style garden detail: scarlet pelargoniums in the window box, painted shutters, and lavenders growing beneath the window.

Above right
Other combinations that evoke the Mediterranean style: drought-tolerant plants, stone terracing and clusters of pots.

The Mediterranean climate and landscape

There is a quality of light that is uniquely Mediterranean: the tingling white dawns that solidify slowly into a cloudless azure; the long, breathless afternoons, stupefied by sunshine; the plunge of the setting sun into the wine-dark sea...

Every summer, millions of tourists descend on the Mediterranean, eager to enjoy the cloudless days and balmy nights. But as they arrive, the plants go into hiding: for them, the prospect of relentless heat and months without rain has no allure. Arrive in spring, however, and it is a different story. Then the barren hills blaze golden with Spanish broom and pink with rock roses; alliums, iris and poppies nod in the meadows; and orchids and asphodel, anemones and Star of Bethlehem flower carelessly by the side of the road. As the temperature soars, the colour drains out of the landscape, to return little by little with cooler nights and autumn rains. The first storms coax autumn crocus and cyclamen into radiant bloom. Then comes the winter – short, wet and frost-free. In Menton, on the French Riviera, the lemons grow all year round, flowering most profusely in mid-winter.

The Mediterranean climate, however, is not confined to countries around the Mediterranean Sea. Similar conditions are found in four other regions across the globe: coastal California,

Above left
The rocky hillsides of the Mediterranean support dazzling displays of colour, such as the electric blue spires of self-sown *Echium pininana*.

Above right
Agapanthus is a bulbous perennial native to South Africa, but has proved so well suited to a variety of Mediterranean climates, that in many countries it has been declared a pest. They dislike winter wet, so a planting like this, with dry mulch round the crowns, is ideal.

central Chile, the tip of South Africa and parts of southern and western Australia. All enjoy mild, rainy winters, followed by hot, dry summers. All are near large bodies of water, which means that temperatures are moderate, varying comparatively little between the winter low and summer high. Of course there are regional variations: Athens, for example, has scorching summers, while San Francisco is comparatively cool and mild. But in general these regions provide a dazzling display of plants that grow lushly for two-thirds of the year, then find various ways of surviving summer drought. (Among them, happily, are vines – these are some of the greatest wine-growing areas in the world.) The sheer diversity is breathtaking: covering just two per cent of the earth's land surface, these Mediterranean regions account for 20 per cent of its plants.

Mediterranean habitats

There are three main types of habitat in the Mediterranean – woodland, *maquis* and *garrigue*. Woodlands are dominated by oaks and conifers, including holm oak, cork oak, the stone pine and maritime pine. *Maquis* has a dense cover of shrubby trees and evergreen shrubs, small-growing oaks and olives. Typical inhabitants are the strawberry tree, Spanish broom, cistus and rosemary. *Garrigue* is more sparse and open, supporting aromatic shrubs such as lavender, sage and thyme. Where garrigue is grazed by sheep and goats, wild flowers thrive, especially spring bulbs such as tulip and iris, crocus and grape hyacinth.

Each region has its own versions of this flora: California has forests of oak and redwood, and scrubby, sun-baked *chaparral*, home to *Ceanothus*, *Rhamnus* and Californian poppy; South Africa has fynbos and Australia has mallee; while in Chile, an area of fragrant matorral lies between the northern desert and monkey-puzzle forests to the south.

As more and more gardeners, from eastern England to southern Australia, face long periods of summer drought, these Mediterranean regions offer hope and inspiration. Why struggle with planting that will wilt and droop in the summer heat, and gobble up precious and expensive water, when there is an almost limitless choice of beautiful plants naturally adapted to do without? Many are already garden favourites, such as tulips, salvias, euphorbias and rock roses, and, by letting them have the conditions they are designed for, they will do all the better for us. As well as resilience, we can enjoy exceptional qualities of colour, foliage interest and fragrance – a Mediterranean garden is not only practical and sustainable in a changing climate, but offers a vivid sensory experience.

Below left
Tulipa sylvestris and rosemary are both fragrant and undemanding plants that will thrive in poor and dry soils.

Below centre
Cistus are native to the Canary Islands and countries bordering the Mediterranean. This rock rose bears beautiful tissue-paper flowers 10cm (4in) in diameter. The five-leaf petals range from white to purple and dark pink.

Below
Scilla peruviana does not come from Peru at all, but from the Iberian peninsula, where it grows in ditches. It does well in shade.

Easy-care Mediterranean plants

Accustomed to poor soils, Mediterranean plants require little or no fertilizer, and are naturally adapted to cope with drought and extremes of weather. So these are perfect plants for a sustainable, low-input approach to gardening.

Born survivors

Mediterranean-climate plants have evolved a whole series of strategies for survival. The first, and most economical, is to complete their life cycle before the summer sun shrivels them up, as in colourful annuals like *Eschscholzia californica*. Other plants retreat underground, sitting out the summer as bulbs, corms and tubers, and flowering in spring or autumn. First come the smallest bulbs – snowdrops, crocus, and tiny irises, followed as the days lengthen by alliums, *Scilla peruviana*, gladioli and foxtail lilies (*Eremurus*), getting larger and showier as they run out of time to reproduce.

The shrubs have no such escape, and must endure four long months without rain. Some have long tap roots (try pulling up fennel!) or fleshy leaves for storing water. Some, like brooms, drop their leaves. But most have leaves that are adapted to reduce water loss, such as the tiny leaves of thyme or the needle-like leaves of rosemary, which reduce the surface area through which moisture can

escape. Others have a thick waxy coating to reduce evaporation, as in olives; or – best news for gardeners – shimmering grey and silver leaves.

Silver and grey foliage

This silvery coloration found in many Mediterranean plants is designed to reflect radiant heat. It is caused by small hairs on the surface of the leaves which trap water, slowing down evaporation and protecting the plant from drying winds. On woolly plants like lamb's ears (*Stachys byzantina*) and *Salvia argentea*, these hairs are visible, whereas in glittering silvers like *Convolvulus cneorum*, the hairs are still there, but reduced to microscopic size. Many silver plants such as artemisias and lavenders also have aromatic foliage – the essential oils help to cool the plant as they evaporate, while the finely dissected foliage of artemisias and santolinas adds to their surface area and garden appeal.

In many Mediterranean gardens these plants are used tightly clipped into balls or shapely mounds;

Below left
The furry foliage of *Stachys byzantina* has a wonderful tactile quality.

Below centre
Ballota pseudodictamnus makes excellent ground cover, or can be trained against a wall.

Below right
Convolvulus cneorum is one of the brightest silvers in the garden, with a smooth, steely sheen.

with the honourable exception of lavender, the flowers are far less interesting than the foliage. Balls of santolina, repeated along a border, bring a gentle rhythm to a garden. Cut off the garish yellow flowers before they open. Furry *Ballota pseudodictamnus* responds exceptionally well to clipping, and can be trained flat up against a wall to resemble an unusually attractive flock wallpaper. The hardier, spikier lavenders, mysteriously known as English lavenders (*Lavandula angustifolia* and *L.* x *intermedia*), make gorgeous low hedges, while the chunkier French or bee lavenders (*L. stoechas*) make better specimen or pot plants. *Artemisia* 'Powis Castle', forming a 50cm (20in) mound of finely cut foliage, is one of those magical plants that makes everything beside it look twice as handsome, so pair it with all your showiest perennials. Another exceptional artemisia is *A. ludoviciana* 'Valerie Finnis', with startlingly bright, deeply serrated leaves, making it a marvellous foil for purple and black foliage. If height is required, go for *Perovskia* 'Blue Spire' with its airy plumes of tiny, violet-blue flowers, or the supremely architectural cardoon (*Cynara cardunculus*), with huge, arching leaves produced

early in the season. Silver-leaved plants make a perfect companion for both pastel and bright flowers, but don't underestimate the simple beauty of repeated low mounds of contrasting foliage – there is no better treatment for difficult, hot, dry banks.

Above
This Provençal garden relies on indigenous plants for a colourful, naturalistic effect.

Tutorial | Propagating lavender

Lavenders are not long-lived, so it is worth building up a supply of new plants. They root readily from cuttings taken in the spring.

The gritty mix in step 1 is made up with equal parts of John Innes no 1 and horticultural grit. Lavender will also root perfectly well in pure sand.

When the plants are established you should begin to prune them as soon as the first flowering is over (see tutorial overleaf).

1 Choose a sturdy shoot that has not flowered. Trim to 5cm (2in) in length, cutting just below a leaf joint, and removing the lower leaves. Prepare a gritty mix (see introduction).

2 Fill 8cm (3in) pots with the potting mix. Use a dibber to make planting holes. Insert the cuttings of lavender round the edge of the pot and firm down the potting mix.

3 Top-dress with a fine gravel to prevent rotting. Place out in a cold frame. Rooting will occur in four to six weeks.

Caring for silver-leaved plants

The secret of success with silver plants is to treat them mean. So site them in a position with full sun. The hotter, drier and hungrier the conditions, the more cheerfully they will respond. Most silver-leaved plants prefer a free-draining, alkaline soil, low in nutrients. The exception is French or bee lavender (*Lavandula stoechas*), which grows naturally on acid soil. Dig in masses of horticultural grit to ensure perfect winter drainage. A sprinkling of potash around the base of your lavenders will improve flower colour; apart from this no feeding is required.

Bushy plants such as *Helichrysum* and *Santolina* need rigorous pruning every spring to stop them becoming leggy. As long as new growth is present at the base, cut back bravely to within 5–10cm (2–4in) of the ground. Chop hardy English lavenders (*Lavandula angustifolia* and *L.* x *intermedia*) back to 23cm (9in) immediately after flowering, even if this means sacrificing late flowers. Overwintering them as sturdy, leafy hummocks, you will keep them going for 20 years or more. Old, straggly plants can be pruned to within a hand's width of the old wood to encourage new shoots.

It is harder to know when to prune French or bee lavenders (*Lavandula stoechas*) because they flower all year long. If there are plenty of shoots at the base, prune hard after the first flowering, then deadhead through the summer. These are not long-lived, but pruning will keep them going for 5 to 10 years. *Convolvulus cneorum* is also pruned in late summer: to ensure a supply of silvery new leaves, cut back each new shoot by two-thirds.

Below
Water-conserving leaf adaptations provide a wealth of foliage interest for the garden.

Tutorial | Pruning lavender

Prune hardy lavenders at the end of the summer as the flowers fade, so they have time to put on a little growth and overwinter as neat, sturdy bushes.

1 Time the pruning of your bushes to coincide with the end of the flowering period when all that remains is straggly stems.

2 Using secateurs (pruners), cut the foliage back to 23cm (9in) or (in an overgrown plant) to a point where you can still see green shoots. Don't cut into the old wood: it will not resprout.

3 Regular pruning will keep plants in good shape and should ensure that the bush does not become woody in the centre.

Creating a Mediterranean garden

There are two ways we can draw inspiration from the Mediterranean – by imitating the landscapes of these regions and drawing on plant combinations that occur in the wild, or by mixing and matching the most exciting plants from all five Mediterranean regions, from coastal California to southern Australia.

The naturalistic approach

This requires us to mimic the landscapes of the Mediterranean, borrowing Nature's own plant combinations to create tough, self-sufficient plant communities that will thrive with minimal attention on difficult sites – a sturdy mix of shrubby trees, silver-leaved shrubs and drought-tolerant perennials (see pages 145–6 for examples). It is an ideal solution for every gardener lacking time, rain or fertile soil. All that is required is good winter drainage – as long as their roots are not waterlogged, these rugged plants will cope cheerfully with rain, hail, frost and snow, and are rarely troubled by pests and diseases.

They will reward your scant care with long seasons of bloom – rosemary, thyme and shrubby salvias flower for months at a time – and fabulous fragrance. The salvias alone offer hundreds of beguiling scents from camphor and eucalyptus to blackberries and spice, or try the pineapple-scented wall shrub *Cytisus battandieri*, bracing junipers or *Cistus ladanifer* with its medicinal, green-pepper scent.

A world of riches

Alternatively, we can look to the many outstanding gardens made in the Mediterranean. Gardens such as Les Cèdres on the French Riviera, nearby La Mortola, and La Mortella in the Bay of Naples have gathered together plants from all five regions of Mediterranean climate and beyond, to amass some of the richest plant collections in the world. The Hanbury Botanic Gardens at La Mortola were founded in 1867 by two brothers interested in the pharmacology of plants, who wished to discover how potentially useful plants might be acclimatized.

Their seaside olive grove soon overflowed with spectacular specimens, including aloes, agaves, palms and citrus trees, while visitors, including Queen Victoria, wrote rapturous accounts of the garden's beauty.

Below
Planted lines of *Lavandula augustifolia* define this garden, directing the eye to the stone hut and gnarled olive tree at the very end.

Tresco's micro-climate supports a wide range of tender, sub-tropical plants, from the South Pacific to the Andes. The warmer climate means that many of these plants can now grow in other temperate climates.

Below
Geranium madarense grows in chalky, loamy or sandy soil.

Today la Mortola is 'twinned' with the Abbey Garden at Tresco in the Isles of Scilly, which nurtures an outstanding plant collection in the miraculously balmy climate within its protective shelter belt, despite its weather-beaten position off the shores of southern England.

These cornucopian gardens, with their sumptuous colour, breathtaking array of forms, and riotous growth, are an invitation to gardeners to throw caution to the winds, and mix and match among the full panoply of

Mediterranean-climate plants. Far from restricting the choice in the garden, the prospect of milder winters and long, dry summers opens up a whole new world of exciting planting. Fabulous plants like *Geranium maderense*, long grown indoors, become a candidate for the open garden where winters are frost-free. With its mass of moodily coloured flowers, fleshy, crimson stems and sultry, deeply cut foliage, it is a magnificent plant – leafing early and in flower for three to four months. The oleanders, bougainvillaea and trumpet creeper (*Campsis*) of our Mediterranean holidays are suddenly viable in sheltered gardens. Honey-scented *Euphorbia mellifera* can be grown with confidence.

The loss of the lawn is amply compensated for by sheets of drought-resistant *Ophiopogon japonicus*, underplanted with starry spring bulbs and autumn crocus. Best of all, the beautiful, sculptural trees of the Mediterranean are now accessible to more of us, including the lovely Judas tree (*Cercis siliquastrum*), strawberry tree (*Arbutus unedo*), pencil-thin cypress, olive and fig.

Creating the Mediterranean look

Of course, plants alone do not make a garden. Mediterranean gardens rely heavily on architecture – steps and terraces, rosy roof tiles, earthy coloured renders, rough stone walls. The same distinctive colours intermingle all over the Mediterranean – ochres, terracottas, rusty reds, a soft browny pink. These translate more easily to more northerly gardens than that other classic combination of snow-white whitewash and bright Matisse blue – the heat-deflecting colours of the Mediterranean islands. Provence has its own cheery palette of reds, oranges, yellows and blues, and with a brightly painted chair, a cushion or two in traditional Provençal fabric and a pot of lavender, you could easily imagine yourself in the south of France. To get the Mediterranean look it is important to use the right sort of paint, with a matt and milky finish. (You may get the best effect by using an interior paint, then sealing with two coats of matt yacht varnish.) Nothing should be too perfect – timber and trelliswork should be rough-hewn, while loose shaley gravels, cobbles or pebble mosaics will be more suitable underfoot than smooth machine-cut paving. Mediterranean style is rough and rustic, and anything slick and glossy would be out of place.

If there is one material above all others that typifies the Mediterranean, it is terracotta, the warm-toned baked clay that reappears in floors and roof tiles, decorative panels, cookware and garden pots throughout the region. For the early Mediterranean civilizations, it was a material as ubiquitous and disposable as plastic is today. But it can also be fashioned with great artistry, as in the beautiful hand-thrown pots that are still produced in parts of southern Spain and Crete. These make a magnificent focal point for any garden. Old oil jars are especially sculptural, if you can get them. But even modern, machine-made pots can be attractive if you choose simple, heavy shapes (do check that they are frostproof), while you can create a convincingly sun-drenched look by topping a wall or a flight of steps with terracotta tiles, and grouping brightly planted pots along its length.

While no temperate garden can ever quite recreate the lambent light of the Riviera, by introducing this kind of warm, rustic detail into your garden, and stimulating your imagination with evocative scents, you will soon be hearing the shrilling of cicadas, and looking out for glow-worms in the velvet night.

Above left
Rough-hewn steps and walls and natural surfaces create a warm, rustic effect.

Above centre
For a Mediterranean style, choose bold paint colours in a matt finish.

Above
A large terracotta pot makes a fine focal point. Leave it unplanted for best sculptural effect.

Plant focus Classic Mediterranean plants

These fragrant, sculptural plants characterize the Mediterranean. They will survive the baking heat and will thrive in any well-drained soil, including those that are poor, thin and rocky.

Olea europaea Olive

The olive is the archetypal Mediterranean tree, grown in the region for at least 5,000 years. The zone of Mediterranean climate is often defined as the region in which olives are cultivated: 90 per cent of the global population of over 1,000 million trees grow there. With its gnarled trunk and slender, ever-grey leaves, the olive makes a beautiful garden tree. The shade it casts is not too heavy, and it responds well to pruning. It is also incredibly long-lived – there are stories of trees over a thousand years old still producing fruit. Olives do best in poor soil, so do not plant them in a lawn where you intend to feed the grass, or in heavily manured beds. Being slow-growing and drought-tolerant, they do very well in pots, which will also allow you to give them some protection against winter wet. (See also page 144.)

Olea europaea

Lavandula Lavender

Lavender is now grown commercially in many countries, but it remains quintessentially the flower of the French Midi, where varieties like *L.* x *intermedia* 'Maillette' are grown for their flowers and essential oils. The Romans used it as a bath oil: the genus name *Lavandula* comes from the Latin *lavare* meaning 'to wash'. In medieval times, it was grown as a strewing herb, flavouring, antiseptic and insect repellent, and was believed to be efficacious against the Plague.

There are 39 species of lavender and nearly 400 cultivars. The hardiest are the spiky *Lavandula angustifolia* and the hybrid *L.* x *intermedia*. *L. latifolia*, fat-headed

Rosmarinus officinalis

Pinus pinea

Lavandula stoechas subsp. *pedunculata*

L. stoechas, *L. s.* subsp. *pedunculata* and velvety *L.* x *chaytoriae* are all frost-hardy. There are also exotic half-hardy lavenders and tender lavenders, such as the toothed *dentata* varieties and the huge-flowered *L.* x *christiana*.

If planting a hedge or path edging of lavender, alternate plants that flower at different times to give you flowers all summer long. Give them a sunny, well-drained site, and never plant them with roses: roses like lots of manure, lavenders hate it – one of them will suffer. (See also page 147.)

Rosmarinus officinalis Rosemary

An essential plant in every garden, and good for dry, infertile soils, rosemary is hardy down to -10°C (14°F), but suffers in wet winters, so needs good drainage to do well. It looks wonderful as a big, sprawling plant with knotty stems, but also takes to clipping into hedges, mounds and balls. The prostrate forms look attractive cascading over steps and walls: small, light blue flowers appear in early spring and last well into summer, often giving a second flush in autumn.

The upright forms tend to flower later, in shades of blue, pink and lilac-white. 'Miss Jessop's Upright' is a neat, tall-growing variety (1.2–1.5m/4–5ft), while 'Corsican Blue' has the loveliest, bright blue flowers. Prune in autumn to keep shrubs compact. Rosemary has many uses, both culinary and medicinal. It is associated with remembrance, and was used for hundreds of years to improve the memory. Good for colds, stress, depression and asthma, it is also an effective hangover cure. (See also page 146.)

Pinus pinea Umbrella pine

The umbrella or stone pine is characteristic of the Mediterranean coast, and is widely planted across the world in areas with similar climates. It has a distinctive, umbrella-like outline, with a single trunk and rounded head; old trees often have several stems supporting a spreading cloud of sharp, grey-green needles. The cones are harvested for pine nuts, while the resin contains turpentine, used as an antiseptic, a remedy for bladder problems, a wax for violin bows, and for waterproofing and varnishes.

This is not a tree for the small garden, since it can grow 25m (80ft) high with a spread of 20m (66ft), but where there is space, and frosts are light and brief, a glance will transport you to the Mediterranean.

Garden plan A fragrant Mediterranean bank

This planting scheme for a hot, dry bank is designed to appeal to the nose as well as the eye, with fragrant herbs and aromatic silver foliage acting as foils for architectural planting.

Honey-scented *Euphorbia mellifera*, shrubby salvia, ornamental marjoram and lavender are all exquisitely aromatic. The planting is rich in texture – felty *Plectranthus*, woolly lamb's ears and bristly mounds of clipped *Santolina* contrast with waxy succulents and feathery fennel. Low, rounded clumps of silver foliage act as foils for dramatic spires of *Echium*, spiky agave, euphorbia and cardoon.

This soft, neutral background allows for vivid splashes of colour: first the blue and lime of *Echium pininana* and *Euphorbia characias* 'Portuguese Velvet', then the violet and crimson of *Geranium maderense* set off by dusky pink and purple *Origanum laevigatum* 'Herrenhausen' (one surging as the other fades), an almost luminous salvia and a delicately coloured fennel that teeters between bronze and grey.

Planting list

1 Honey spurge (*Euphorbia mellifera*)

2 Cardoon (*Cynara cardunculus*)

3 Salvia (*Salvia* 'Black Knight'). For a hardy salvia, substitute ruby-red pineapple sage (*Salvia elegans*)

4 Parry's agave (*Agave parryi*)

5 Lamb's ears (*Stachys byzantina*)

6 Cotton lavender (*Santolina chamaecyparissus*)

7 Silver plectranthus (*Plectranthus argentatus*). For a hardy alternative, use felty *Ballota pseudodictamnus* or a softer artemisia.

8 Ornamental marjoram (*Origanum laevigatum* 'Herrenhausen')

9 French lavender (*Lavandula stoechas* 'Marshwood')

10 Madeira cranesbill (*Geranium maderense*)

11 Evergreen spurge (*Euphorbia characias* 'Portuguese Velvet')

12 Echium (*Echium pininana*)

13 Fennel (*Foeniculum vulgare* 'Smoky Joe', but any bronze fennel would work in this scheme)

14 Purple aeonium (*Aeonium purpureum* 'Zwartkop'. You could substitute *Aeonium arboreum* 'Atropurpureum'.

Euphorbia mellifera is chosen for its honey scent and year-round structure.

The cardoon has dramatic silver leaves and giant thistle flowers.

Euphorbia 'Portuguese Velvet' is very neat in habit, with beautiful steely-blue, mildew-resistant foliage.

This salvia has beautiful, deep purple flowers, but is tender.

Echium pininana is a characteristic plant of the Mediterranean. When happy, it will seed itself about.

Origanum laevigatum 'Herrenhausen' is a long-flowering herb that offers both colour and fragrance.

Lamb's ears have the most strokeable of foliage – but also bear attractive flowers.

The hardiest of the agaves, *Agave parryi* has beautiful markings on the leaves as it unfolds

Project **Planting a thyme pavement**

Rather than make a conventional herb garden, you can integrate rosemary, sage and fennel into the border, and grow fragrant thymes in a path or pavement. They will thrive in these conditions, which so closely mimic their natural habitat.

You will need

Pegs

String

Ground paint

Shovel

Hand-held plant compactor

Levelling pegs

Scalpings

Paving slabs

Mortar

Rubber-headed hammer

Spirit level

Selection of thyme plants

Potting mix

Large-sized gravel, such as Cotswold stone chippings (used here)

Thyme choices

Creeping *Thymus serpyllum* varieties spread most quickly, but are quite soft-textured. For the centre of the pavement, where they are likely to be stepped on, choose robust varieties like *T.* 'Faustini' or a lemony *T.* x *citriodorus* that will not break. In a warm, well-drained site, they will bulk up quickly, and every stroll along your pavement will smell delicious.

1 Choose a sunny, open site and mark out the area of the pavement with pegs and string. String can be a nuisance when you are digging, so mark out your design with ground paint when you are happy with it.

2 Dig down to firm subsoil, allowing for a 10cm (4in) layer of scalpings. Tamp down the subsoil before the scalpings go on – it is worth hiring a hand-held plant compactor for a large area.

3 Lay out the slabs, leaving wide gaps, and photograph to record the pattern before removing them. Drive in levelling pegs at regular intervals and fill with scalpings to the level of your pegs. Compact to make a level surface.

4 Lay large dollops of mortar in the centre and at each corner of the slab. Position the slab and tamp down with a rubber-headed hammer, or protect the slab with a piece of wood. Use a spirit level to check that each slab is level.

5 Lay out the thymes. A selection of different coloured varieties will give interest. Remember to water the plants well before you plant. Make up a very gritty potting mix because, even with the scalpings all around them, thymes need good drainage.

6 Excavate a planting hole to twice the size of each plant, working the scalpings into the potting mix. The creeping varieties grow quickly, but you may need to plant two or three of the bushy varieties together for instant impact. Top-dress with large-sized gravel.

The gravel garden

For many of us, summer drought has become a regular problem, with hosepipe bans and watering restrictions wreaking havoc on our gardens. So rather than pine for verdant lawns and billowing herbaceous borders, which can only be sustained through arduous labour and a profligate use of water, we need to think about gardening in a new way – one that will be more sustainable, ultimately more successful, and just as beautiful.

Gravel gardens are cheap and easy to make, and simple to maintain: the deep gravel mulch suppresses weeds and conserves moisture. And as we become more aware of the ecological aspects of gardening, a garden that requires no chemicals, no power tools and little or no water, seems all the more attractive. Here is a style of gardening suited to today's hectic lifestyles – adaptable, low-maintenance, and highly appropriate for small urban and suburban plots.

There is no better choice for a hot, dry site, where water is in short supply. It is ideal for new-build sites, where gardens, beneath a cosmetic layer of topsoil, are usually full of builder's rubble. And, with maintenance cut to a minimum, there will be plenty of time to sit and relax in the sunshine.

Opposite
The gravel garden offers a sustainable, low-input way of gardening in a changing climate.

Above left
A palette of drought-tolerant, Mediterranean plants provides just as much interest in terms of colour and texture as a traditional herbaceous border, without all the bother of watering and staking.

Above right
These Californian poppies (*Eschscholzia californica*) create luminous patches within the pastels and gravel that surround them.

Inspiration for the gravel garden

Today's gravel gardens draw on two very different sources of inspiration – parched natural landscapes with their successfully adapted flora; and the ancient gardens of the East. While totally different in their appeal, both offer practical solutions for modern gardens.

Much of the aesthetic of the modern urban garden dates from the 1930s, and the sleek, uncluttered lines of Modernism. The architects of the thirties were influenced in their turn by the gardens of Japan, with their emphasis on simplicity, asymmetry and sculptural form. Garden-making tends to follow architecture at a respectful distance of about 50 years, so it is not until around the 1980s that we see the

1930s aesthetic seeping out into the garden – a minimalist look that uses plants as living sculpture and abandons the pocket handkerchief lawn in favour of sweeps of gravel.

The tradition of gravel gardening is, however, very ancient. The Chinese were laying out gardens well before 1000 BC using rock and stone in symbolic patterns. The garden became a representation of the universe in miniature, an idea absorbed into Japanese culture from around the 7th century AD. In this tradition, sand, gravel and slate came to represent water, flowing from miniature 'mountains' or arranged in 'seas' in which were placed 'islands' of carefully selected rocks.

Above
This Japanese dry garden at Tofuku-ji has raked circles of gravel representing the eight rough seas, hills of moss as sacred mountains and rocks as islands, all forms derived from ancient Japanese myths.

Zen Buddhism arrived in Japan in the 12th century, and with it came perhaps the most minimalist garden style the world has ever seen. The Zen masters created breathtaking gardens from stones and gravel: in its purest form, no plant cluttered the *kare-sansui* or dry garden, except the odd clump of moss. The most celebrated and intriguing of these works is the 15th-century Ryoan-ji in Kyoto – a temple garden about the size of a tennis court that consists of just 15 rocks, arranged in groups within a simple rectangle of perfectly raked, white quartz.

These were not gardens as we understand them, as places to walk, eat or play. They were designed as aids to contemplation, and places of spiritual refreshment. This quality of stillness is a huge inspiration for modern minimalist garden-makers such as Vladimir Sitta in Australia, Christopher Bradley-Hole in Great Britain and Shodo Suzuki in Japan. In their gardens, planting tends to be sparse and highly sculptural in form, set off by pale gravels and meticulously laid paving. These tranquil spaces work especially well in urban situations, as harmonious extensions to the uncluttered, modernist home.

However, gravel gardening can also be adapted to a quite different style, altogether more exuberant and theatrical, which combines a sparse vocabulary of well-placed plants with hard-edged, colourful materials such as glass, steel and polished concrete. Even the smallest, most inhospitable space can be enlivened with swirling compositions of rock and slate, upended rocks and coloured glass mulches, paired, where conditions allow, with sculptural grasses, topiary or dramatic succulents. Ideal for the forgotten spaces among factories and office blocks, this energetic style has many possibilities for the adventurous urban gardener.

Below left
At the Canadian embassy in Tokyo, a dry garden with natural rocks and gravel pays homage to the past while also displaying the cutting edge of modernity.

Below right
Crushed blue glass gravel forms the surface of a raised bed planted with diminutive grey succulents and drought-resistant herbs.

Natural landscapes

A quite different approach to the gravel garden is the ecological one. Here the garden recreates the conditions of a natural landscape, whether a rocky Mediterranean hillside or a pebble beach, using drought-tolerant plants and carrying the associated ease-of-care benefits. The delight of this approach is that you can create this style of garden anywhere, with any quality of soil.

Drought-tolerant gardens

In the ecologically inspired garden, gravel is the natural companion of plants that thrive in conditions of low fertility and low rainfall. As our summers become hotter, our winters drier, and rainfall more unpredictable, this becomes a more rewarding and a more responsible way of gardening.

Prospect Cottage, the garden of the film director Derek Jarman (1942–94), was made on a shingle beach in the shadow of a power station on the south coast of England. By using indigenous plants that would thrive in these windswept conditions, such as sea kale (*Crambe maritima*) and *Santolina*, poppies and pinks, and combining them with attractive flotsam and jetsam, Jarman created one of the most widely admired gardens in Europe.

A gravel garden is the obvious choice if you live by the sea, while if you garden inland, a beach garden is an easy effect to recreate – with a mulch of beach cobbles, a sprig of sea holly (*Eryngium*) and a lobster pot or two, you can be anywhere from Cornwall to Cape Cod.

While England is seen as a country of rain and fog, the county of Essex, on its eastern side, has less rainfall than parts of Greece, and is experiencing more extreme weather conditions, with summer temperatures regularly exceeding 30°C (86°F) and long periods of summer drought. These conditions have made this region a hotbed of horticultural

Below left
Derek Jarman's garden on England's south coast was made round a fisherman's cottage on a shingle beach, using pebbles, driftwood and endemic plants.

Below right
In this New Zealand garden, low-maintenance ground cover and grasses are paired with architectural lupins and cardoons to great effect.

experiment where, in recent years, many people have abandoned the traditional English garden, with its endless requirement for water and labour, in favour of various forms of dry gravel gardening.

Foremost among these is Beth Chatto's pioneering garden, now a model for gardening in summer-dry conditions. Her site is a former car park: a third of a hectare (three-quarters of an acre) of dry-as-dust, compacted soil, made up of sharp stones, sand and gravel to a depth of 20m (62ft). There is only 50cm (20in) of rainfall a year. Chatto decided that this garden would not be watered, and set about selecting a palette of drought-tolerant plants that would not only thrive, but deliver year-round interest in these unpromising conditions.

The no-water garden

Beth Chatto's garden draws its inspiration chiefly from the Mediterranean, with gently curving beds laid out each side of a sinuous, central path. There is no separation between path and bed – an important feature for a natural-looking gravel garden. Structure is provided by cider gum (*Eucalyptus gunnii*) and mountain gum (*E. dalrympleana*), *Juniperus scopulorum* 'Skyrocket' and Mount Etna

broom (*Genista aetnensis*), with a rich tapestry of Mediterranean shrubby plants and bulbs around their feet. *Yucca gloriosa* 'Nobilis', bold variegated agaves and the silvery candelabras of *Verbascum bombyciferum* make striking punctuation points, while sheets of *Verbena bonariensis*, the butterfly blooms of *Gaura lindheimeri* and rivulets of poppies and *Nigella* add fluttering colour and movement.

Gravel gardens are sometimes accused of being sparse and sterile, but this planting is every bit as rich as a traditional herbaceous border, and shows how a modern, sustainable garden can be full of colour and interest, using tiers of planting and contrasting plant forms. In fact, many traditional border favourites are drought-tolerant and suitable for the gravel garden, such as alliums, oriental poppies, bergenias and euphorbias. While alliums and poppies are not long in flower, their interest is extended by their lovely seedheads. Bergenia is good for foliage contrast and autumn and winter colour, while nothing can beat euphorbias for year-round colour and structure. These plants are watered thoroughly on planting, and then left to take their chance – but you can help them along a little while they establish.

Above left
In Beth Chatto's garden in eastern England, a palette of drought-tolerant, Mediterranean plants provides just as much interest in terms of colour and texture as a traditional herbaceous border, without all the bother of watering and staking.

Above right
The naturalistic dry garden at Hyde Hall in Essex shows plants from all around the world that will thrive in areas of low rainfall.

Below
Hyde Hall's dry garden is
never watered and is
managed organically.
It demonstrates the wide
range of plants, such as
grasses and *Teucrium
hircanicum,* that will thrive
in dry conditions.

Creating perfect drainage

It is perfectly possible to create a gravel garden on heavier soil. While Beth Chatto's garden is naturally gravelly, just a few miles away is Hyde Hall, a show garden for Britain's Royal Horticultural Society, which sits on a seam of heavy Essex clay. Perched on an exposed hilltop, shrivelled by drought in summer and battered by Siberian gales in winter, Hyde Hall is not an easy place to make a garden. None the less, it is the site of an inspirational dry garden, which, once again, is never watered. Plants adapted to tolerate drought need excellent drainage, so in order to give them the conditions they require, the dry garden has been built up into a series of hillocks, constructed with rubble from demolition sites, and punctuated with rocks of gabbro. (Gabbro is not a quarried rock, but detritus dumped on the landscape by retreating glaciers.) The effect is of a natural rocky outcrop, with winding paths meandering between huge boulders to allow close inspection of well over 4,000 plants, from every continent except Antarctica.

Soil and planting

The dynamic design of Hyde Hall is a model for heavier soils and less well-drained sites, with plants set on mounds or in raised planting pockets, and placed with their crowns proud of the soil to keep them dry. If you want to follow this model, careful soil preparation is vital – before planting, mix in plenty of sharp sand or horticultural grit (up to 50 per cent in volume), and plenty of organic matter, to aid drainage. It is safest, as well as most economical, to use small plants – they will establish more easily, and you will be amazed how quickly they bulk up. They may also flower earlier than you expect: the gravel mulch acts as a storage heater, warming the soil up quickly in spring.

While preparing the site is hard work, the finished garden is wonderfully easy to maintain. The compactly growing plants need no staking and are rarely divided. Dried flower stems and grasses can be left through the winter to provide food and shelter for wildlife, then cut back hard in spring. With a thick layer of pebble mulch, weeding is minimal, consisting mainly of restricting over-enthusiastic self-seeders.

Garden jewels

While Jarman, Chatto and Hyde Hall offer ideas for designing your whole garden based around gravel, there are other kinds of gravel gardening that can be enjoyed in the tiniest space. Scree gardens

mimic the conditions of alpine scree (the loose, weathered rock debris that appears at the base of slopes and crags), and can be made in any raised bed, by filling the base of the bed with a deep drainage layer of rubble, topping up with a very gritty potting mix, and top-dressing with gravel or shale. It is the ideal way to display delightful, small, drought-loving plants that would be overwhelmed by the more vigorous planting of the gravel garden. Suitable plants include *Diascia*, *Phlox* and saxifrages, miniature narcissi and *Sisyrinchium*, *Rhodohypoxis* and exquisite species tulips.

There has been a fashion for growing these jewel-like plants in old kitchen sinks or home-made tufa troughs. They deserve better. A planting bed in the top of a wall provides an attractive option, or the gently sloping roof of a shed or storage box, or even parallel lengths of piping, arranged at different angles. At the University of Utrecht Botanic Gardens in the Netherlands, roof slates have been piled into strata resembling natural rock formations, while broken paving stones have been recycled into three magnificent spheres, 1.5–2m (5–6½ft) tall, planted with sea pink (*Armeria*), Whitlow grass (*Draba*), houseleek (*Sempervivum*) and saxifrages, with tiny *Asplenium* ferns colonizing the shadier parts.

Alpines have very similar needs to succulents – lots of light and sunshine, perfect drainage, and protection from winter wet. Both are used

to growing in poor, shallow soils. So the rockery project shown on page 96 would work just as well for alpines. Or just grow them in shallow bowls and mass these lovely plants together like gems in a jeweller's shop window.

Above
At the Utrecht Botanic Gardens discarded materials have been cleverly recycled to provide a dramatic home where alpines can be enjoyed at eye level.

Far left
Here, old broken paving slabs provide conditions similar to a natural rock face.

Left
This succulent display, in a length of old clay pipe, would be easy to replicate at home.

Planning your gravel garden

Before settling on a site, take time to think about the practicalities – not just the aspect of the site and how you want it to look – but details like drains, cables, and access to water and electricity for any features you may wish to install.

Choosing the right site

Whatever style of gravel garden you prefer, you will need a site that receives direct sun for as many hours of the day as possible, away from the shade of trees or buildings. Less hardy plants may also need some protection from the wind. Before you begin, consider whether you will need access to any drains, cables or septic tanks. Will you need to take mowers or barrows across the garden to reach your compost bin or shed? (Pushing these across gravel is very hard work!) How will you stop gravel migrating into your lawn if you have one?

Cotswold stone
The warm honey tones of Cotswold stone are sympathetic to most plantings. Pair with shrubby plants that would naturally grow on Mediterranean hillsides, such as iris or cistus, beautiful bulbs like *Scilla peruviana*, or striking architectural plants like *Melianthus major*.

Grey slate
Chippings in grey or purple slate will set off silver- and dark-leaved plantings particularly well, creating a dramatic modern effect. Ideal with silvery *Artemisia* and *Convolvulus cneorum*, wine-coloured smoke bushes (*Cotinus*) or aptly named *Sambucus* 'Black Lace', with its almost black, feathery foliage.

Plastic edging strips are flimsy and ugly, while metal ones are hugely expensive. Could a line of bricks, wood or stones do the job? Are you going to use a geotextile membrane beneath the mulch? And what kind of gravel should you choose?

Choosing your gravel

Gravel is made from natural stone chippings of many kinds, ranging in colour from white and buff to red, brown and black. Choose local stone for the most natural effect. The size of stone will also affect the look. Larger gravel has some advantages – it doesn't stick in your shoes and travel into the house; cats find it less comfortable to 'visit'; and babies seem less inclined to eat it. Plants also seed in it less readily, but you may not consider this a benefit.

While gravel is available by the bag from DIY stores and garden centres, it is more economical to buy by the tonne sack from an aggregates or builder's merchant. They can help you calculate how much you need: your mulch should be at least 5cm (2in) deep. Wash the gravel before applying to remove any excess lime, and keep a record of your choice: unless you are using a membrane, you will need to top it up in future years.

Beach shingle
Worn smooth by the sea, beach shingle (legally sourced, of course) is kindest to small knees and hands. Plant up with sea holly (*Eryngium*), Californian poppies (*Eschscholzia*) and smaller grasses and decorate with driftwood or other found beach objects for a relaxed, seaside effect.

Pale monochrome
Gravels in pale monochrome are best for Japanese raked effects, as they show the shadows better. They also look fantastic paired with black, or with contrasting dark paddlestones. Use these gravels to show off sculptural plants such as acers, bamboos or cloud-pruned azaleas.

Garden plan An island planting

The planting in this island plan, inspired by Hyde Hall in Essex, is arranged on a mound, highest at the back and falling towards the front and left-hand side. The design is punctuated with large rocks. The planting scheme uses the European fan palm (*Chamaerops humilis*), a dramatic structure plant, and many grasses such as Indian rice grass, switch grass and giant feather grass that ripple in the wind. All this movement is balanced with mounds of shrubby plants such as *Santolina* and *Helianthemum* and solid clumps of blue-green euphorbia. It is a look that is both beautiful and practical in any exposed site.

Planting list

1 European fan palm (*Chamaerops humilis*)

2 Indian rice grass (*Oryzopsis miliacea*)

3 Russian sage (*Perovskia* 'Blue Spire')

4 Switch grass (*Panicum virgatum* 'Heavy Metal')

5 Bear's breeches (*Acanthus spinosus*)

6 New Zealand tea tree (*Leptospermum scoparium*)

7 Spurge (*Euphorbia characias* 'Portuguese Velvet')

8 Iris of your choice

9 Sea holly (*Eryngium bourgatti* 'Picos Blue')

10 Golden oat grass (*Stipa gigantea*)

11 Feather grass (*Stipa tenuissima*)

12 Wall daisy (*Erigeron karvinskianus*)

13 Rock rose (*Helianthemum* 'The Bride')

14 Cotton lavender (*Santolina chamaecyparissus* 'Lemon Queen')

Smaller plants are arranged around the margins of the planting to appear as if they have self-seeded round the rocks (which indeed they will, in time).

The lightest of grasses, including *Stipa* and *Oryzopsis* contrast with the large-leaved planting behind.

Chamaerops and *Acanthus* form massy, large-leaved backstop plantings.

Plant focus Grasses for the gravel garden

Supremely architectural, low-maintenance and with a long-lasting season of interest, these drought-tolerant grasses are ideal for both the naturalistic and the minimalist garden. (See also page 146.)

Calamagrostis x *acutifolia* 'Karl Foerster' Feather reed grass

A strong, vertical element like this forms a good foil to the low, shrubby plants that thrive in the gravel garden. Although *Calamagrostis* generally inhabits dampish soil, 'Karl Foerster' performs better in hot, dry conditions, growing stronger stems that stand up gamely to rain and wind. It starts into leaf early in the spring, forming a tall, dense clump. The panicles emerge in late spring, shooting up to 1.5m (5ft) high and bearing bronzy-purple flowers that dry to a rich honey colour and last robustly through autumn into the winter.

Elymus magellanicus Blue wheat grass

The bluest of all the blue grasses when grown in full sun, this beautiful deciduous grass comes from Tierra del Fuego at the tip of South America, where it thrives on stony beaches in ferocious winds. Forming generous, rounded clumps of metallic foliage, 40–50cm (16–20in) high, it carries flower spikes the same colour as the leaves from mid- to late summer.

Oryzopsis miliacea Indian rice grass

Delicate panicles arch upwards and outwards from clumps of shiny green leaves, surrounding the plant in a shimmering golden halo that lasts well into winter. This grass will reach 60cm (2ft) in height.

Elymus magellanicus

Calamagrostis x *acutifolia* 'Karl Foerster'

Panicum virgatum 'Heavy Metal'

Stipa gigantea

Oryzopsis miliacea

Stipa tenuissima 'Pony Tails'

Panicum virgatum 'Heavy Metal' Prairie switch grass

Panicum varieties once covered the North American prairies. A really strong, upright-growing grass (reaching 1–1.8m/3–6ft tall) that melds harmoniously into mixed plantings, the grey-blue leaves take on a steely sheen when grown in full sun, then turn dramatically butter-yellow in autumn. From mid-summer to early autumn, large, open panicles of purple-green create a haze of colour above the foliage.

Stipa gigantea Golden oat grass

No wonder this grass has become so popular – how can you fault it? The delicate, oat-like flowers last for months (early summer to late autumn), and the stems are graceful but sturdy, rising from a neat basal clump of fine evergreen foliage. Reaching 2m (6½ft) and more in a sunny, well-drained spot, this is the loveliest of specimen plants for the gravel garden. To show it at its best, position it where it can catch the low, evening sun.

Stipa tenuissima 'Pony Tails' Feather grass

Elegant and compact at 30cm (1ft) tall, this invaluable grass associates cheerfully with all gravel garden plants, its creamy, soft-as-a-feather seedheads softening spikier neighbours, blurring the outlines of rocks, and bringing soft, swooshing movement to the garden. A short-lived perennial, it seeds around when happy, and can usually choose its site more artfully than we can.

Preparing your gravel site

Just like decorating, the success of the gravel garden depends on thorough preparation. There's no doubt preparing the soil is hard work – but once established, the gravel garden will be easy to maintain.

Creating layers

Begin by transplanting any plants you to intend to reuse, then clear the site of perennial weeds. The quickest method is by spraying with glyphosate. Alternatively, cover the site with black polythene or landscaping fabric for a whole growing season (it will then require replacement). Clear the dead weeds, then, if you have time, let the plot rest for two to three weeks. A bountiful crop of annual weeds will appear in the disturbed soil, which you can then hoe off.

If you intend to remould the site, remove all topsoil and set it aside, while you reshape the subsoil. If the area drains poorly, you may need to install a drainage layer before replacing the topsoil (an 8–10cm/3–4in layer of 20mm/¾in stone will do the trick) or even lay a drainage pipe to a soakaway.

Next, get to work on your topsoil. For a heavy clay soil, mix 25 per cent topsoil with 25 per cent organic matter and 50 per cent horticultural grit. For a light loam, mix 50 per

cent topsoil with 40 per cent organic matter and 10 per cent grit. For a sandy or gravelly soil, forget the grit and mix 60 per cent topsoil with 40 per cent organic matter. These additions will open up clay soils and improve the moisture-retaining capacity of the free-draining ones. If you choose naturally drought-resistant plants, they will need no further feeding, as their natural habitat is low in nutrients.

If, however, you are choosing sculptural rather than ecological planting, this is your one and only chance to incorporate a slow-release fertilizer. When replacing your topsoil, the final height should be about 5cm (2in) below the adjoining ground, to leave enough room for your gravel mulch without spilling over.

Right
Weathered timber planks make an attractive feature in a shingle gravel garden, creating a secure, textural transition across pebbles with small clumps of planting to give colour and texture.

Below
A cross section of a gravel garden. The topsoil will need more or less improvement, depending on your location and the plants you want to grow. The top dressing can be made from stone chippings, pea or beach gravel – use local stone for the most natural look.

Top dressing of gravel

5cm (2in) gravel mulch

Geotextile membrane

Improved topsoil

Drainage layer of 8–10cm (3–4in) stone

Subsoil

Tutorial | Planting through a geotextile membrane

If you are planning a new area of garden, a geotextile membrane will save you a lot of work, but there are some drawbacks. For example, it makes it more difficult to dig up and split plants that have bulked up, or to move them about. If you have not previously improved your topsoil, you will need to incorporate horiticultural grit, organic matter and possibly slow-release fertilizer as you dig out your planting hole – it will be your last chance.

1 Using a sharp knife, cut a cross shape through the membrane where you mean to plant. You will now have four triangular flaps. Fold them back under the membrane to expose a neat square of earth. Dig out the planting hole.

2 Water both the plant and the hole well before planting. This will make sure the moisture is where it is needed: trapped below the layer of mulch at the roots. Add superphosphate if required, to promote root establishment. Plant firmly.

3 If you are using larger stones, keep a small amount of finer gravel for mulching round the crown of your plants to leave room for growth. Small plants may also need the protection of an upturned flowerpot as you mulch them, to stop them getting buried.

Weedlings or seedlings?

A geotextile membrane made of woven plastic effectively blocks weed growth, while allowing rain to pass through it into the soil. It is ideal for new areas of garden, which may take some years to be completely cleared of weeds. It also separates the gravel mulch from the earth below, keeping it clean and preventing it from sinking into the soil. If, however, your soil is heavy, the gravel working its way down over time will help to open it up and improve drainage. You may also prefer to do without the membrane if you wish to encourage self-seeded plants – there is no better seedbed than fine gravel. (Remember this also applies to weeds!)

If you do decide to use a woven membrane, pin it down at regular intervals with tent pegs or wire pins (you can make simple wire loops out of old coat hangers) before setting out your plants. Remember not to plant too closely – plants bulk up quickly and you will want some gravel to remain visible. Soak each plant and water the hole before planting. Then after planting, water in generously once more. Even drought-loving plants will appreciate some moisture while they are establishing. But after the first year, you can put your watering can away.

Below
Happy plants spread surprisingly rapidly, so space them widely to start with, or the gravel will soon disappear.

The dry river bed

This imaginative garden feature, creating the illusion of water, is ideal where water is scarce. It is most effective when it appears to have been created by the elements, rather than artfully placed.

Virtual water

According to classical Japanese geomancy, a stream should enter the garden from the north or east, and leave flowing westwards, to wash away any evil spirits inhabiting the place. The substitution of gravel for water freed Japanese garden-makers from the constraints of nature, and they became highly skilled at arranging stones to imitate the motion of flowing water. The 'virtual' river bed remains a favourite feature of the Japanese garden, often flowing from a *karedaki*, or dry waterfall, through dry rapids into pools, designated by smooth, rounded stones. The movement of water is replicated in paddle stones, lying flat where water would run slowly and rising to stand on end where water would surge and eddy, or splash up against the rock. There is even a special stone, the *rigyoseki*, which represents a mythical carp flowing upstream.

A rivulet of coloured gravel can be a simple way to enliven a formal courtyard garden. But a dry river bed also offers a pleasing way to integrate a gravel garden into an existing scheme. Inspired by a visit to the Greek island of Delos in the 1960s, English plantswoman Joyce Robinson created a gravel 'river' at Denmans, near the south coast. Her garden now belongs to internationally acclaimed garden designer John Brookes, but Robinson's 'river' still loops lazily down a gentle slope, with irregular sizes of stones and occasional slabs of rock as much as 1.8m (6ft) long. The planting appears random – an effect Brookes achieves by allowing plants (especially verbascums) to self-seed, then editing them to create a wild look.

A dry river bed, created from large boulders, 'banks' of rock, pebbles and gravel, should suggest water only temporarily absent – water that could reappear with a sudden storm. It will look most effective sited on gently sloping ground, with grasses or small bamboos simulating the sound and movement of a stream, or drought-lovers like euphorbias, *Cistus* and scrubby thymes recalling the dusty, sun-baked watercourses of Corsica or Crete.

Below
The gravel river at Denmans in Sussex, England. The natural effect is created by encouraging plants such as *Verbascum olympicum* and *Sisyrichium striatum* to seed themselves about.

Plant focus Beautiful self-seeders

Plants that seed themselves around give just the right, natural, look to gravel and river-bed gardens, and because they germinate a few at a time, they are guaranteed to give you a good long display. Should they seed too enthusiastically, then it's not much trouble to pull up the ones you don't want. (See also pages 148–9.)

Erigeron karvinskianus Wall daisy
This tiny (10cm/4in) prostrate daisy will seed itself into the most inhospitable cracks and crevices, and grow into a large, frothy clump whose flowers last all summer long. It is, however, a wilful plant, that will not grow from seed where you want it. The answer is to buy the plant in a pot, and place it near the wall, pavement or rock fissure you wish it to seed into. When left to its own devices, it will usually oblige.

Eryngium giganteum 'Miss Willmott's ghost'
This aristocratic biennial version of the sea holly (*Eryngium*) bears large, tight flower cones like tall, silver thimbles, each sitting on an elegant ruff of spiky bracts, and reaches 90cm (3ft) in height. It is popularly known as 'Miss Willmott's ghost', after Ellen Willmott (1858–1934), a notoriously prickly Edwardian plantswoman, who made a habit of scattering the seed in gardens she visited. It is curiously hard to grow from seed under controlled conditions, so the best idea is just to toss a handful of seed into your river bed, or to buy one or two plants in flower. Then the secret of success is total neglect. Leave it alone and you will soon have plantlets everywhere.
E. bourgatii is a smaller (45–60cm/18–24in), perennial version from the Pyrenees, with flower cones and stems of electric blue. The variety 'Picos Blue' is especially vivid. It has really beautiful, dark foliage, marbled with strong, white veins. Be sure to pull up surplus seedlings promptly because they grow colossal tap roots.

Nigella damascena Love-in-a-mist
Annuals should not be overlooked in any gravel garden. Once established, this easy-going plant will come back year after year, especially if you leave the attractive seedheads in place, rather than cutting back immediately after flowering. Just sow it wherever you want it to flower, and thin out any excess seedlings when they start to emerge.

Verbena bonariensis

Erigeron karvinskianus

Eryngium giganteum

Verbascum olympicum

Verbascum olympicum Olympic mullein
Architectural plants of the highest order, these evergreen biennials will seed themselves freely along your riverbank. In the first year, they offer elegant, silver rosettes of felty foliage. In the second, they erupt into giant candelabras of bright yellow flowers, lasting well from mid-summer onwards. They reach a height of 2m (6½ft). *Verbascum bombyciferum* is slightly smaller and more reliably evergreen.

Verbena bonariensis Verbena
The most useful 'see-through' plant in the garden, this short-lived perennial from South America is a marvellous foil for mound-forming shrubby plants. It throws up long, angular, square-shaped stems 1–2m (3–6ft) tall that bear little topknots of deep purple flowers from mid-summer well into autumn. Just four or five plants should ensure a graceful purple haze dancing above your planting for years to come.

Nigella damascena 'Alba'

Project Making a dry river bed

This project uses large rockery stones, walling stone, shale and gravel. A pale colour has been chosen to look dusty and parched. If your garden is green and lush, the dark sheen of grey-green slate paddlestones may sit more harmoniously.

You will need

Spade

Geotextile membrane, to cover the area required

A selection of stones: rockery stones, wall stones, shale and gravel

Drought-tolerant plants included here are *Libertia peregrinans, Euphorbia characias* 'Portuguese Velvet', *E.* 'Blackbird', *E. myrsinites, Festuca glauca, Stipa gigantea, Stipa tenuissima, Elymus magellanicus* and *Betula jacquemontii* (silver birch tree).

Using stones and rocks

• Stones should always be laid with any strata lines running horizontally – because this is how they would occur in nature. Where stones occur close together, make sure that the strata lines match up – this will give the impression of a continuous rock feature.

• Ensure that your stones come from a sustainable source. Never use water-worn limestone – this is extracted from endangered limestone pavement habitat – and remember that taking stones from your local beach is both illegal and unsustainable.

1 Clear the site and mark out the stream. It must have a logical start and end, flowing to a destination such as an area of gravel. Dig out a channel 20–30cm (8–12in) deep, using the spoil to create raised banks.

2 Cover the area with a geotextile membrane. Position your largest stones at the turning points of the stream. Either build up the stone around them, or cut away the membrane and bury the stones by a third of their depth.

3 Use resilient drought-tolerant plants including low, evergreen grasses like *Festuca glauca* scattered along the stream bed, *Elymus* and stipas for movement and tough libertias and euphorbias for year-round colour.

4 Use the next size down of stones to define the course of the river, arranging them irregularly, so they look as if they have been hurled by the water's force. Set out your plants to look as if they have seeded randomly along the banks.

5 Once you know where everything is going to go, you can start filling in with smaller sized stones, using a mixture of sizes for the most naturalistic effect and packing the gaps between the larger boulders to conceal the membrane.

6 Soak the plants, prepare the planting site and plant through the membrane (see tutorial on page 79). Surround the plants with stones, and finish with a scattering of fine gravel. Scatter your remaining stones randomly along the centre of the river bed.

The desert garden

We tend to think of deserts as empty places, blasted by a cruel sun. But, in reality, the desert teems with wildlife, and is second only to the rainforest in its abundant biodiversity. So, rather than blotting out these delicate ecosystems with alien plants and a garden style that derives from a different climate, can we not find a way of gardening that celebrates the austere beauty of the desert and the richness and strangeness of its unique flora?

In this kind of garden, statuesque native plants can provide magnificent living architecture, while the sun is changed from enemy to ally, casting bewitching shadows that give the garden depth and drama. The native planting calls in hummingbirds and songbirds, filling the garden with colour and life. Precious water, no longer squandered to keep suffering plants alive, may be carefully recycled in refreshing rills and chutes. This kind of desert garden, in its boldness and simplicity, shows how gardening in extreme conditions can actually enhance rather than restrict the creativity of the gardener.

Opposite
Houseleeks are hardy alpine succulents that will make a showstopping statement in any garden – and will happily survive outside all year in a dry situation.

Above left
In common with most *Puya* species, *P. chilensis* offers convenient perches for pollinating birds to sit and reach the nectar.

Above right
As European summers become warmer, succulents such a aloes and agaves can be successfully grown outside.

Gardening in desert conditions

Desert gardens expand our horizons. They teach us to forget conventional notions of what makes a garden – including lawns and green leaves – and think differently about how we can make beautiful outdoor spaces in harmony with their environment.

Deserts occupy about one-fifth of the earth's surface, and are generally defined as regions where the annual rainfall is less than 25cm (10in). Worse still for the plants, this meagre rainfall tends to fall in irregular bursts, while temperatures fluctuate wildly. The sun beating down through the clear desert skies causes daytime temperatures to soar, but with no insulating cloud cover to contain the heat radiating from the ground, scorching days may be followed by cold, even frosty, nights. In Nevada, for example, daily temperature fluctuations of 60°C (140°F) are not uncommon. So drought is by no means the gardener's toughest challenge: only plants well adapted to these extreme conditions can hope to survive.

This may explain why some of the world's most famous desert gardens are not in desert areas at all. Both the Huntington Botanical Gardens and the Ruth Bancroft Garden are in California; César Manrique's Jardin de Cactus is in Lanzarote; while Monaco's Jardin Exotique overlooks the Mediterranean Sea. These areas all have a climate that is Mediterranean, indicating how well desert plants can be grown in more temperate conditions.

Above left
The cactus garden at the Huntingdon Botanical Gardens in California is the most extensive in the world. The more temperate conditions allow the widest possible range of desert plants to thrive.

Above right
A garden in Phoenix, Arizona, designed by Steve Martino. He exploits the sculptural qualities of native desert plants to create striking garden pictures.

Living sculpture

Today, the Huntington is the world's largest desert garden, cultivating some two-thirds of all known cacti and succulents in innumerable glasshouses and nearly five breathtaking hectares (12 acres) of ornamental garden. There are aloes from South Africa, euphorbias from Madagascar, aeoniums from the Canaries, and bromeliads from Peru. From Mexico come pincushion cacti, spiky agaves and teddy-bear-shaped opuntias. And from Baja (Lower) California come what are surely among the weirdest plants on the planet: the alien-looking boojum tree (*Fouquieria columnaris*) and the creeping devil cactus (*Stenocereus eruca*), which worms its way westwards over any object (growing at one end, dying at the other), and rooting itself as it inches along. Ruth Bancroft, meanwhile, seduced half a century ago by a single succulent, now grows some 2,000 species of desert plants in a verdant San Francisco suburb.

Many of these plants would not survive in the searing heat of the Arizona desert, where landscape architect Steve Martino makes his gardens. Martino aims to create beautiful and sustainable outdoor living-spaces that flow seamlessly into their desert surroundings. With less than 18cm (7in) of rainfall and summer temperatures regularly approaching 40°C (104°F), it makes sense to use plants native to the Sonoran or nearby Chihuahuan deserts. These include ocotillo (*Fouquieria splendens*), brittlebrush (*Encelia farinosa*), agaves and cactus, chosen not only for their resilience, but also for their outstanding sculptural qualities. Martino often places these plants against solid walls rendered in deep, glowing hues, creating a richness of colour and texture in the garden, as well as a surface on which shadows can play. The plants are widely spaced to display their architecture to full advantage, but this is also how desert plants grow in the wild.

When Martino first started out in the 1970s, it was considered highly eccentric to forsake the water- and energy-guzzling, palm-fringed gardens of the day in favour of minimalist gardens filled with plants that many considered weeds. No nurseries stocked desert plants, so he had to collect the seed himself and get them grown for him. But, today, Martino's spare and naturalistic style is widely admired as a practical and sustainable response to gardening in the desert, and a model for many gardeners who find themselves battling with increasingly arid conditions. As all of us experience greater extremes of heat and cold, deluge and drought, we would do well to follow Martino's example of seeking out garden-worthy native plants adapted to survive such conditions.

Below
At the Kotoske Garden in Phoenix, Arizona, Steve Martino places desert plants in containers to bold architectural effect.

The ingenuity of desert plants

The desert garden is a testament to the cleverness of plants, celebrating the many ways they have devised to survive with little or no water. These remarkable adaptations offer a fund of decorative interest to the gardener.

Below left
The ornamental spines of the Mexican golden barrel cactus (*Echinocactus grusonii*) are designed to reflect light and to direct moisture towards the roots.

Below right
The leaves of *Agave parryi* are so tightly packed, they leave a distinctive pressure pattern on the waxy leaf surface as they unfurl.

Strategies for survival

There is no end to the ingenuity of desert plants. There are plants that draw moisture almost entirely from the air, as in the fog-desert areas of Baja (Lower) California. There are plants such as *Ariocarpus* with roots that pull them underground in order to shelter them from the scorching sun. Desert annuals bide their time as seeds in the soil, germinating and growing only after heavy rains. And while in cool climates, deciduous plants drop their leaves in response to falling temperatures, many desert plants respond in this way to drought, growing leaves again after rain. The ephemeral leaves of the ocotillo (*Fouquieria splendens*), for example, generally reappear three days after a shower. Other plants, such as the aptly named living baseball

(*Euphorbia obesa*), have no leaves at all and photosynthesize through their stems or trunks. Many plants, such as yuccas, agaves and prickly pears (*Opuntia*), only open their stomata at night when evaporation rates are lowest. But by far the most common survival strategy is succulence, which means storing a supply of water in stems, leaves, roots or all three.

Succulent characteristics

As gardeners, we use the term 'succulent' to denote fleshy-leaved plants such as crassulas or sedums. But, botanically, cacti are also succulents, storing water in their stems. Many cacti have dense coverings of wool, hairs or bristles to protect them from the sun, while the golden barrel cactus (*Echinocactus grusonii*)

can blow itself up and down like a balloon to regulate its surface area. While cacti rarely have leaves (these have developed into ferocious spines), the leafy succulents are characterized by water-saving leaf arrangements – tight rosettes or fans that protect a part of each leaf from exposure.

It is this intricate geometry that makes desert plants so attractive as garden plants, whether on the tiny scale of houseleeks (*Sempervivum*) or the gargantuan rosettes of the mighty American agaves. Their interesting textures are the result of various water-saving adaptations, producing surfaces which may be waxy, leathery, bristly, pebbly and knobbly, even curiously felty, such as *Kalanchoe beharensis*, which feels as though it were cut out of carpet tiles.

Below left
The rosette arrangement of *Aeonium atropurpureum* reduces the total amount of leaf surface that is exposed to the sun.

Below right
Echeveria tolimanensis has a very sculptural form with fat, rigid leaves which act as water-storage organs.

Growing cacti

A cactus bed makes an eye-catching feature, whether as permanent planting in hot and arid conditions, or a summer display in a cooler clime. Several forms are easy to grow and hardier than is generally supposed.

Making the most of cacti

It is winter wet rather than cold that is the enemy of cacti. In places where temperatures rarely fall below freezing, many can stay outside all year long, provided the drainage is good. In temperate climes, most cacti and succulents will grow outside very happily in pots during the warmer months of the year, while agaves and opuntias can endure quite severe frosts if given waterproof winter shelter.

A cactus bed makes an eye-catching feature: simply sink the plants in terracotta pots into a raised bed filled with sand or grit, then top-dress with fine gravel. Alternatively, in frost-free areas make up a free-draining mix of one part grit and one part peat-free potting mix to two parts of loam-based potting mix. Choose a sunny position and ensure the drainage is flawless by filling the bed with crocks to a third of its total height. If you can, raise the bed above ground level; if not, leave plenty of gaps for water to escape. While most cacti will survive for years without food and water, they will not actually grow; to keep them fat and happy, feed sparingly with slow-release fertilizer and water occasionally, wetting the sand rather than the plants (they will absorb what they need through the porous terracotta) and letting it dry out completely between waterings. Once back in winter quarters, just one watering a month should suffice.

Cactus combinations

Cacti look best with other cacti, or counterpointed with spiky yuccas or agaves. Tall columns of *Cereus* combine well with the rounded shapes of barrel cactus (*Ferocactus*) or the 'teddy-bear' outline of prickly pears (*Opuntia*). For the indoor garden, both *Mammillaria* and the many forms of *Gymnocalycium* make round balls rarely exceeding 15cm (6in) in height, bearing brilliantly coloured flowers.

Below left
It is the variety of forms that makes the cactus garden so appealing – contrasted, in this Australian garden, with cascades of juicy succulents.

Below right
Opuntia robusta is one of the larger growing prickly pears, making rounded pads up to 50cm (20in) in diameter. It is hardy to -8°C (18°F).

Garden plan A summer cactus bed

It is the interplay of sculptural forms that makes a display of cactus so interesting. Generally endemic to the Americas, cacti have spread successfully across the globe, including Australia, Hawaii and the Mediterranean. More moderately sized versions can be grown anywhere where they can be protected against frosts. The planting scheme here will work equally well as larger permanent plantings in a desert climate, as shown below, or in temperate climates using smaller, pot-grown specimens.

Planting list

1 Prickly pear (*Opuntia phaeacantha*)

2 Pillar cactus (*Stenocereus*)

3 Chapparal yucca (*Yucca whipplei*)

4 Golden barrel cactus (*Echinocactus grusonii*)

5 Sedum or trailing ice plant (*Lampranthus spectabilis*)

6 Century plant (*Agave americana*)

Opuntia phaeacantha is a slow-growing prickly pear, reaching a height of about 1m (3ft) tall, with large pads up to 30cm (12in) long by 20cm (8in) wide. *O. robusta* grows much larger, but can get floppy. Fallen or damaged pads make delicious treats for tortoises.

Stenocereus are distinguished by their ribbed, columnar form and nocturnal flowers. There are many species available, ranging from centimetres to metres in height.

The slow-growing golden barrel cactus, five of which have been planted here, starts as a ball and gradually becomes more barrel-shaped.

Yucca whipplei has finely toothed, narrow leaves that grow slowly to 1m (3ft).

Lampranthus is an easy-to-grow, fast-spreading, ground-cover succulent with greyish triangular fingers of foliage and long-lasting, daisy-shaped flowers in vivid shades of red, pink, orange or purple.

Choose a large and a small specimen of variegated agave such as 'Marginata', which has leaves with yellow or white stripes on the margins (shown here), or 'Striata', which is showier, with irregular yellow stripes over the whole leaf.

Sumptuous succulents

While cacti may be something of an acquired taste, few gardeners need persuading of the virtues of succulents. They have superb architecture and enormous presence in the garden, are easy to propagate, and require virtually no maintenance, as they are designed by nature to feed and water themselves.

Choosing suitable succulents

Mainstays of the desert garden, succulents deserve to be far more widely used. The smaller echeverias and crassulas make fine container displays in the small patio garden where their intricate detail can be appreciated, while showy architectural specimens add just the right note of theatre to a minimalist courtyard or stately Italian urn. The larger succulents have long been favourites with Mediterranean and gravel gardeners, who often use the dramatic outlines of agaves, aloes and yuccas as punctuation points among softer planting. Most yuccas and agaves from higher altitudes such as *Agave parryi* and the spectacular *A. montana* are

frost-hardy when mature, although younger plants will require some protection. There are several aloes that will survive light frosts, including *Aloe aristata*, *A. arborescens*, *A. striatula* and the magnificent *A. ferox*. As with cacti, perfect drainage is the key to survival. Where winters are mild but wet, it is worth constructing an open-sided polythene shelter to keep rain out of the crowns, but, as aloes flower in winter, you may enjoy them more in the glasshouse.

Succulent sensation

As well as being fine companions, succulents look magnificent when grouped together, where their variety of colour, texture and form can be

Below left
Agaves are striking feature plants that will always produce a bold effect.

Below right
The succulent rockery at Tresco shows just how much variety this plant group has to offer.

appreciated. At Tresco, on the Isles of Scilly, succulents drip from rocky outcrops and scramble over stony banks. The colour and vitality of the display is astounding, with agaves the size of a small car sprouting from a rock-face; jellybean leaflets of *Senecio*; aeoniums in shades of green, blue and pink or deep, glossy mahogany; and the starfish forms of aloes in purple, orange and crimson. Another dimension is added when they flower. Ferocious aloes produce delicate, bell-like blooms;

lampranthus carpets the ground in papery magenta daisies; while the aeoniums sprout long, broccoli-like stalks which erupt into sulphur-yellow flowerheads.

Frosts here are rare, light levels high, and the soil virtually devoid of nutrients. This makes for a fair approximation of desert conditions, despite cool summers and high rainfall. For gardeners with less space and less favourable conditions, superb results can be achieved by growing succulents in pots, massed together for summer displays.

Above left
Succulents offer exceptional interest for little effort. Small ones make exquisite displays for pots, boxes and hanging baskets.

Above right
The thrusting flower spikes of mature aeoniums make a dramatic feature in the garden.

Tutorial | Propagating rosette-forming succulents

Many succulents, such as echeverias, aeoniums and sempervivums, are easy to propagate by potting up the offsets that develop round the parent plant. These offsets divert energy from the parent, which will grow much stronger if you remove them.

It is quick and easy to increase your stock of succulents to fill a bowl or hanging basket. Or if you plant your babies directly into small clay pots, these look great lined up on a wall or windowsill.

1 Cut away a rosette from the parent plant using a sharp knife or secateurs (pruners). (You may simply be able to uproot a small plant without cutting.)

2 Remove any withered leaves. If your plantlet has any roots, repot it straight away. If you have cut the stem, leave it for a week or so to callus over.

3 Plant into a barely moist loam-based potting mix, combined with an equal quantity of grit. Top-dress carefully with gravel and water sparingly until roots form.

Spectacular spikes

Spiky plants bring a rush of energy to the garden and there is none more useful than the yucca family to break up softer planting. Or, for maximum impact, try exotic *Beschorneria* or vicious desert *Puya*.

Below left
Where plants that can prick or stab are not an option, choose softer but no less dramatic *Beschorneria yuccoides*.

Below centre
Yucca rostrata makes a highly architectural specimen with its narrow foliage and pale, interestingly textured trunk.

Below right
Puya chilensis, which can reach a height of 2–3m (7–9½ft), has great impact, but requires plenty of space in the garden.

Yuccas

The Spanish dagger (*Yucca gloriosa*) is a familiar specimen in seaside gardens, with its spires of creamy, bell-shaped flowers and sharp, blade-like leaves, but *Y. whipplei* is a hardier plant (10ºC/50ºF) with more elegant blue-green foliage. Where height is needed, *Y. aloifolia* (Spanish bayonet) forms a trunk up to 1.8m (6ft) tall, while *Y. rostrata* will make a chunky tree 3–4m (10–13ft) high.

Creating levels of drama

A softer, more textured effect can be achieved with *Dasylirion serratifolium*, which forms a ball of narrow, shiny leaves with grassy tufts at the end, resembling a fibre-optic lamp. But for sheer showmanship, you can't beat *Beschorneria yuccoides*. From yucca-like foliage springs an outrageous pink flower spike, some 1.8m (6ft) long, dangling with red and green flowers. All these plants are members of the agave family, but, unlike true agaves, do not die after flowering.

Equally arresting are the puyas, bromeliads from the Chilean Andes, which throw up towering flower spikes in titanium shades of yellow, blue and green. While the *Puya chilensis* flower resembles an airborne pineapple, turquoise-flowered *P. alpestris* has more pronounced spikes providing a perch for pollinating birds. Both are reliably hardy, but require plenty of space because of their fiendish thorns. These point both inwards and outwards, so small creatures that steal into the clump find themselves unable to escape. The animals eventually die and decay, providing a handy slow-release fertilizer.

Plant focus Show-stopping succulents

It is the beautiful leaf-forms of so many succulent plants that make them so attractive, and such striking focal points in the garden. Flowers are a bonus, but when they appear they are often magnificent.

Agave Century plant

This group of perennial succulents originates from the deserts and mountains of Mexico, and other parts of North and Central America. They have rosettes of overlapping leaves armed with vicious thorns along their edges and formidable spines at the tip. They are worth the pain of handling, however, for their incomparable architecture in the garden. These plants are monocarpic, meaning that they flower and fruit only once in their life cycle, after which they die, leaving new side shoots to grow on. The common name of 'century plant' derives from the erroneous belief that they live 100 years before flowering. In reality, the average lifespan is more like 8 to 12 years, though cosseted container specimens seem to last much longer, and can achieve heroic proportions. In favourable conditions, *Agave americana* can reach 1.8m (6ft) in diameter, with a flower-spike soaring to 8m (26ft); the variegated forms are smaller and less hardy. *A. montana* is another giant, with rounded grey leaves, beautifully marked and toothed and edged with burgundy thorns. *A. parryi* is smaller, with a spread of 60cm (24in), but is equally handsome and a reliable choice for temperate gardens, where mature specimens, kept dry in winter, can withstand temperatures as low as -12°C (11°F).

Aloe candelabrum

Aloe plicanthus

Aloe

The invaluable *Aloe vera* is one of a huge genus of succulents which form rosettes of thick fleshy leaves, varying from low, grass-like plants to lofty trees. This foliage can be highly decorative, as in *A. mitriformis* and scarlet *A. dorotheae*, while *A. plicatilis* has its leaves piled up vertically in the manner of a menorah. Most have vicious prickles along the leaf margins. While their fascinating evergreen architecture is their chief value to the gardener, the flowers are also superb, *A. ferox*, *A. candelabrum*, *A. andongensis*, and *A. spectabilis* being especially showy. On each flower petal are three thin, green lines (honey guides) that channel pollinators (usually birds) towards the nectar. Aloes respond well to a fertile soil, and grow happily in containers, where they can reach impressive sizes.

Aeonium cuneatum

Aeonium

These evergreen, rosette-forming perennials are native to the Canary Islands, the Mediterranean and North Africa. They are very similar to echeverias in appearance, but typically bear their rosettes on woody stems, while instead of dainty blooms, huge pyramids of yellow, pink or white flowers are produced on alarming elephantine trunks that shoot from the centre of the rosettes.

A. cuneatum is a soft green, edged with pink, which can grow as fat as a cabbage and seeds freely when happy. *A. tabuliforma* is the size of a dinner plate and almost as flat, its complex geometric pattern emphasized by the microscopically fine hairs that fringe each leaf tip. The purple forms of *A. arborescens* 'Atropurpureum' and *A.* 'Zwartkop' are particularly striking, the foliage growing darker, the hotter and sunnier its spot. (See also page 148.)

Agave americana, growing with *Aeonium arboreum* 'Atropurpureum'

Project Creating a succulent rockery

Your old, broken pots can be recycled to create an ideal environment for displaying smaller succulents, creating an unusual feature for a hot spot in the garden. The plants will thrive in these spartan conditions which mimic their natural habitat.

You will need

Broken crocks

Horticultural grit

A selection of succulents such as echeverias, sedums, aeoniums, crassulas and small aloes

A loam-based potting mix with plenty of horticultural grit mixed in

Decorative gravel for top-dressing

Arranging the succulents

• Use shallow planting depths, with little potting mix, as this mimics how succulents grow in nature.
• When top-dressing, take care not to get gravel caught between the leaflets as it is hard to get it out! Cover each plant with an upturned flower-pot as you work, if necessary.
• Many garden centres sell multiple packs of succulents, ideal for a feature such as this.
• If your garden is frosty, you will need to bring in the topmost aloe for the winter. The remainder of the plants can survive to -10°C (14°F) in this position, if protected by a polythene cover to keep out the wet.

1 Select a suitable site, such as this sunny corner. Backed by heat-retentive bricks, this is one of the hottest spots in the garden and offers some shelter from the rain, so it is ideal for desert plants.

2 Backfill the site with broken crocks and horticultural grit to form a base on which you can plant. Use small shards to block any holes from which the potting mix might escape.

3 Work out your arrangement while the plants are still in their pots. It is easier to change your mind that way, without causing any damage. Then take a photograph as a reference, or plant up a little at a time.

4 Remove all the plants and fill the framework with a free-draining, low-nutrient potting mix. Combine equal measures of a suitable loam-based potting mix and horticultural grit or perlite.

5 Plant up the pots, then top-dress them with a decorative gravel. The small, round gravel used in aquariums looks just right in this arrangement.

6 As a final flourish, add a scattering of extra plants at the lip and beyond the edge of the pot, to look as if they have self-seeded. Dribble the top-dressing over the edge of the pot and merge it into the surrounding surface.

The bush garden

It was only natural that the first European settlers in Australia and New Zealand, as far away from home as it was possible to be, should seek to recreate under a harsh, alien sun, the verdant lawns and fulsome flower borders they had left behind. Only gradually did they come to appreciate the extraordinary beauty of the flora that surrounded them – a palette of plants quite unlike any other in the known world, which could thrill and enthral with its boldness and vigour, and extraordinary diversity of foliage and form.

As water shortage has become an ever more serious problem, a new generation of environmentally sensitive Antipodean garden-makers is enthusiastically embracing this tough and resilient plant heritage, and developing a more sustainable and contemporary style of gardening. Their experiments, as successful in suburban plots as in wilderness bush gardens, show how these dramatic and dynamic plant families can offer inspiration for adventurous gardeners all over the world.

Opposite
The cabbage palm *Cordyline australis* flowering in a New Zealand seaside garden. Early settlers ate the crowns of the plant as a vegetable, giving rise to its common name.

Above left
The tree ferns of Australia and New Zealand have taken the world's gardeners by storm, especially the fabulously fronded *Dicksonia antarctica*.

Above right
The black seedheads of New Zealand flax, *Phormium tenax*, silhouetted against the sky.

A unique evolutionary inheritance

When, 200 million years ago, the great southern continent of Gondwanaland started to break apart, the largest part to drift away became the modern continent of Australia. Here, its vegetation continued to evolve in isolation, developing many unique and spectacular genera. Western Australia, in particular, has developed one of the richest floras on the planet, with over 8,000 species – second only to the Cape in its diversity. In the islands of New Zealand, a similar explosion of endemic species occurred: over 80 per cent of New Zealand's native plants occur nowhere else.

What this means for the gardener is a huge range of totally distinctive plants. And now that so many of us are experiencing milder winters and longer, hotter summers, many of these plants, previously considered borderline tender, can be grown successfully in our gardens.

In fact, Australia and New Zealand encompass a very wide range of climate zones, ranging from arid desert to tropical rainforest to snowy alpine meadows, so there are plants to suit every garden situation. Such vast diversity rather makes a nonsense of generalizations; none the less, it is fair to say that these countries offer an unparalleled selection of plants whose interest lies not so much in their flowers (although there are eucalypts, bottlebrushes and banksias that all have spectacular blooms) as in their dynamic and dramatic shapes, and in their endlessly varied and fascinating foliage. While a handful of these plants, such as cordylines and tree ferns, have become fashionable in recent years, there are many, many more equally excellent plants deserving of a place in our gardens, still begging to be discovered.

Above left
In this New Zealand bush garden, the variety of colour and texture inherent in native grasses is exploited to great effect.

Above right
Spiky cordylines and fans of *Dicksonia antarctica* bring drama to the garden.

Opposite
The beauty of this New Zealand bush garden lies in the contrast of the leaf forms. The flowers on the golden *Libertia peregrinans* are a temporary bonus.

Architectural plants

The bold, satisfying shapes of architectural plants provide essential structure in a garden, adding drama and strength to the design, and guiding your eye around the space. Australia and New Zealand offer some of the best.

Creating dramatic outlines

Do you ever look at a part of your garden, and feel that is not quite working? Then follow the suggestion of plantsman Noel Kingsbury, and take a picture of it in black and white. That way, purged of colour, you will see at once where the problem lies. Does your eye roam vaguely over the garden, rather than being guided to a focal point? Does your border offer an interesting interplay of shapes and textures, or is it just a mass of woolly blobs? It is all too easy, seduced by a show of colourful flowers, to forget about the form of a plant. But flowers are soon over, while the foliage and overall shape of a plant offer more lasting pleasures.

It is here that the native plants of Australia and New Zealand excel. The spiky, sword-like forms of phormium, cordyline and astelia bring instant drama, with their powerful sense of energy and uplift. They contrast well with low, hummocky mounds and light, branching skeletons, such as the graceful small tree *Amelanchier lamarkii*, or a large bronze fennel (*Foeniculum vulgare* 'Purpureum'). The hebe family provides, in a variety of sizes, rounded shapes as neat as a clipped box ball. *Corokia cotoneaster*, with its complicated interlacing branches, is aptly named the 'wire netting bush', and what, for sheer impact, could compare with the great arching fronds of the Tasmanian tree fern *Dicksonia antarctica*? Unless, perhaps, it comes in the bizarre juvenile form of the slow-growing lancewood (*Pseudopanax ferox*), its long, ferociously toothed leaves dangling from a slender stem like the spokes of a half-open umbrella?

Pseudopanax is one of a fascinating group of New Zealand plants which alters completely in appearance as it ages, growing eventually into a spreading, candelabra-shaped tree. It has been suggested that this adaptation developed in order to prevent the young trees being eaten by moas, giant, ostrich-like birds that inhabited the primeval forest. *P. crassifolius* is the best form – one of many small trees or large shrubs offering sculptural, multi-branched silhouettes.

Make your choice of architectural plants, bearing in mind the conditions in your garden and what protection, if any, you can give them over winter. Use them to supply the 'bones' of an informal garden, as hedges and topiary do in formal Italian designs. As all these plants are evergreen, the framework will remain in place throughout the year.

Below
This shady London garden gives a taste of two worlds; it includes the antipodean visitors *Phormium* and *Cordyline*, along with classic cottage plants, astrantia and foxgloves, in the foreground.

Tutorial **Using spiky plants**

Though their chief value lies in the year-round impact of their sculptural foliage, both *Phormium tenax* and *P. cookianum* are also magnificent in flower, with flower stalks soaring up to 4m (13ft) and handsome seedpods. Try these tips to get maximum effect from them in your garden. Other spiky plants, such as cordylines and astelias, can be used in the same way.

1 Creating a visual exclamation mark
The eye seizes on definite forms sooner than amorphous ones. Rosettes of sword-like foliage provide a highlight in the border, contrasting with restful rounded shapes. Repeating these forms will give a strong sense of rhythm. (See above.)

2 Creating a full stop
The bulk and strength of *Phormium tenax* makes a good full stop at the end of a border, or a backstop for lighter planting.

3 Creating a focal point
Dramatic foliage makes a compelling focal point. It will lead the eye to the end of a vista – a cordyline in a stone urn is a classic terminus for a formal avenue. It will also draw the eye away from less attractive elements.

4 Creating a sense of direction
Strong forms give direction in the garden. Rather than take a flight of steep steps down a slope, a succession of phormiums can mark the way for a downhill or zig-zag path, anchoring it into the garden. (See above.)

5 Using similar colours
Combine striped cordylines or phormiums with variegated pittosporum in the same shades – not a scheme for the faint-hearted! (The tiny leaves and contorted stems of corokias also make a pleasing background.)

6 Combining similar forms
Combine phormiums with *Stipa gigantea* or other tall grasses with a similar spiky outline – the heavy and gossamer-light version of the same form work brilliantly together.

7 Creating a jungle effect
Phormium tenax tolerates some shade, and grown through giant leaves like *Fatsia japonica* or *Gunnera manicata* creates a striking jungle effect. (See above.)

8 Using a pair of sentinels
A pair of sentinels either side of the path will swiftly draw the eye along it. They can also mark an arbour or a doorway. Choose smaller plants – perhaps silvery *Astelia* 'Silver Spear' – or the central object will be overpowered.

***Phormium* species**
P. tenax has stiff upright leaves which can reach 3m (10ft) high; *P. cookianum* is smaller (up to 2m/7ft) and laxer in habit. Both will spread to at least 1m (3ft) in width, and both prefer conditions with a little shade.

Easy-growing plants

Their undemanding habits make Australasian plants ideal for spaces that are shared or always on show, like front yards, community gardens or school grounds, as they give huge visual impact with minimal maintenance.

Below
This holiday house garden in New Zealand receives only sporadic maintenance, but still looks spectacular.

Year-round impact
These plants provide all-year-round colour and structure, while requiring little in the way of maintenance: no pruning, staking or dead-heading is needed. They associate well with each other, hence the growing popularity of 'New Zealand gardens' in Britain and the Mediterranean. On the other hand, where space is at a premium, a single, well-chosen architectural plant against a simple backdrop of ivy or an attractive wall can be all it takes to make a spectacular front garden.

Adaptable evergreens
The plants described in this chapter are ideal for warm and sheltered urban and suburban gardens, or for gardens in milder coastal areas. The majority will tolerate surprisingly low temperatures (phormiums can survive temperatures as low as -12°C/10°F), as long as they do not also have to endure winter wet. So, a well-drained site is essential. If this is not an option, you can still enjoy the moisture-loving tree ferns (*Dicksonia antarctica*) and the surprisingly resilient New Zealand cabbage palm (*Cordyline australis*), while carex and cortaderia will grow more lushly on a damper site. Most shrubs and trees cope admirably with summer drought (except the tree ferns again), but will need watering during their first year in order to help them get established.

Many of the smaller-leaved plants, along with leathery-leaved plants such as the familiar *Brachyglottis greyi* and *Griselinia littoralis,* are more wind-tolerant than is generally supposed, making them ideal for seaside plantings. Nearly all thrive on poor, thin soils, and many grow cheerfully in that most difficult situation in the garden, dry shade. Among these heroic plants are the phormiums and *Pseudopanax*; *Griselinia, Corokia, Coprosma* and *Olearia*; all the libertias, *Dianella* and *Elymus solandri,* and the useful ground-covering plant, *Acaena*. So gardeners all over the world may look to the New World and give thanks.

Fabulous foliage

Whatever your local conditions, the sheer variety of Australasian foliage plants, from a range of climate zones, offers a lively combination of shapes and textures that will form a brilliant evergreen backbone for the garden.

Contrasting foliage

Plants with large or distinctively shaped leaves show well against neat, dense foliage, such as hebes and *Lophomyrtus*. The glossy, lime-green leaves of *Griselinia littoralis* make an elegant backdrop for soft-textured plants like grasses, or bristly ones like bottlebrushes (*Callistemon*). Both these are resilient, undemanding plants, and are particularly useful in coastal and windy gardens. Contrast glossy with matt – too much gloss is unsettling. Small-leaved plants like pittosporum, despite a sheen on the leaf surface, read at a distance as matt, and make the ideal foil for showier subjects. *Pittosporum tenuifolium* is the most obliging of plants in a temperate or warm climate – fast-growing, neat in habit, and responding well to clipping into cones and mounds – an informal form of topiary that gives an extra dimension to the border.

Plants with strong shapes and shiny leaves are the loudest presence. These need to be tempered with softer neighbours, such as hairy-leaved plants, which appear soft and felty, finely divided ferns, or soft, hazy grasses. Also think about placing plants to enjoy their foliage in close-up: the curious origami folds of *Hebe epacridea*, the lovely crinkled outlines of the mountain holly (*Olearia ilicifolia*), or the leaves of the lacebark (*Hoheria populnea*), which look as if they have been cut out with pinking shears.

Permanent structure

Because the vast majority of these plants are evergreen, just a handful of successful combinations are all you need to provide a strong permanent structure for a garden. For example, start with a backstop of spiky *Phormium*, with a loose dome of *Pittosporum* to one side, and to the other a brushy *Grevillea*. Add a neat round ball of *Hebe pinguifolia* in front, a swirl of carex to the side, balanced perhaps by some big, shiny leaves of bergenia, and here is a satisfying combination of shapes and textures that will hold together all year round – before you have thought about foliage colour or flowers. With these in place, you can then ring the changes with seasonal plantings of bulbs and perennials – the ideal solution for every gardener frustrated by lack of time.

Above
A *Pittosporum tenuifolium* hedge surrounds this Californian town garden. *Pittosporum tenuifolium* is adaptable and fast growing, and offers a wonderful array of different leaf forms and colours, from silver and gold to pinky-green and purple.

Splashes, spots and stripes

With such an abundance of form and texture to play
with, colour is a bonus. Once again, the bush
garden provides a plant palette encompassing every
shade of green and grey, silver and gold, purple and
plum, and adaptable plants to suit many climates.

Drought-tolerant coprosmas vary from gold to
chocolate and crimson, with the added contribution
of blue or white berries. The grasses range from
mahogany (*Uncinia uncinata*) and copper (*Carex
buchananii*) to clearest blue (*Elymus solandri*). The
new growth of hakeas (with their dry, sunny climate
preference) is a deep, rich bronze, while many
gardeners will already be familiar with *Pittosporum
tenuifolium* 'Tom Thumb', whose young shoots of
soft lime-green contrast weirdly with mature foliage
of deep purple. Loveliest of perennials, the libertias,
offer delicate, white flowers set off by fountains of
foliage from the darkest of greens (*Libertia ixioides*)
to a glorious, glowing bronze (*L. peregrinans*), a
show-stopper in the winter garden. They grow in the
shade, tolerate temperatures down to -15°C (5°F)
and withstand prolonged frost and snow.

No perennial offers such an astonishing
rainbow of colours as the phormiums, ranging
from the glowering grey-green of *Phormium tenax*
to cultivars of brilliant gold, cream, flamingo-pink
and apricot, deep purple, maroon and even black,
with many extravagantly striped in a mixture of
hues. More gentle colour combinations may be
enjoyed in the variegated pittosporums, with leaves
delicately bordered, splashed and spotted. Some
colours are so subtle that they defy description: the
Cootamundra wattle, *Acacia baileyana* 'Purpurea',
has foliage tinged with purple, red, silver and blue, a
wonderful specimen for a sheltered courtyard.

Aromatic leaves

Foliage can offer another delicious dimension to the
garden. Fragrant plants are best appreciated when
grown close to a door or window, or by a path
where you brush the leaves as you pass.
Eucalyptus, callistemons and leptospermums are
members of the fragrant myrtle family. There is
nothing like a mature eucalyptus in the midday sun
for clearing the nasal passages, while various
varieties of tea tree (*Leptospermum*) are sold as
natural mosquito repellents, the lemony scent so
delightful to us being apparently repugnant to the
midge. The many forms of the Australian mint bush
(*Prostanthera*) are all deliciously aromatic, while the
grevilleas have a delicate honey scent.

Plant focus Evergreen and easy-going

Essential elements of the Antipodean bush garden, these easy and fast-growing plants are an asset to gardens everywhere, providing beautiful form and colour all year round, and often fragrance as well. Some become large, so place carefully, or be willing to prune.

Pittosporum tenuifolium 'Silver Queen'

Pittosporum
This is an essential foliage plant, much prized by flower arrangers, which can be clipped into hedges or topiary specimens. Try *P.* 'Garnettii', a fast-growing column of grey and white, which flushes prettily pink in autumn. Countless cultivars of the kohuhu (*P. tenuifolium*) have been selected for their crinkly leaves and lovely patterns of variegation, such as 'Abbotsbury Gold', 'Silver Queen' and the gorgeous 'Irene Paterson', whose leaves emerge cream, fade to a soft green splashed with white, then turn a dusky pink. (See also page 153.)

Eucalyptus
These unfussy, fast-growing trees are deservedly popular, combining elegant form, fragrant evergreen foliage and attractively patterned stems. The silvery adult leaves are generally willowy, while the young leaves are round and more brightly coloured. Many species, such as the cider gum (*E. gunnii*) and the tingiringi gum (*E. glaucescens*), can be maintained as a bush of juvenile foliage by cutting back to the base every few years. The snow gum (*E. pauciflora* subsp. *niphophila*) has a beautiful dappled trunk. The chalk-tolerant small-leaved gum (*E. parvifolia*) is smaller and hardier, with attractive peeling bark. (See also page 152.)

Pittosporum 'Irene Paterson'

Graceful grasses
New Zealand offers a particularly fine selection of easy evergreen varieties of grass. *Anemanthele lessoniana* (formerly known as *Stipa arundinacea*) thrives in sun or shade, turning rich tawny bronze in autumn. *Carex testacea* transmutes through tones of green and orange, and, like the leatherleaf sedge (*Carex buchananii*), looks spectacular grown in sweeping swathes through the garden. *Chionochloa rubra* (red tussock grass) and *C. flavicans* both make elegant, rounded clumps, while *C. conspicua* (plumed tussock grass) bears airy panicles on arching stems up to 1.8m (6ft) high. Even more striking is the majestic pampas grass, *Cortaderia splendens*: up to 6m (20ft) tall in flower, it makes a powerful statement in the garden.

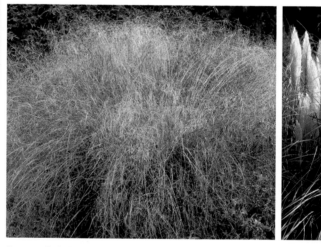

Anemanthele lessoniana

Cortaderia splendens

Eucalyptus bark

Eucalyptus gunni

Garden plan A New Zealand island bed

Resilient New Zealand natives are combined in this low-maintenance but high-impact planting. It offers a wonderful display of year-round colour and texture, which is especially good in autumn and winter when the large grasses retain their feathery plumes. The dense growth of the *Podocarpus nivalis* and the wiry stems of *Muehlenbeckia astonii* provide a lively contrast with the many different shapes and textures of the spiky plants, from the bold blades of phormium to the silky grasses.

The fine, weeping leaves of this *Chionochloa rubra* range from greeny brown to russet. The flowering stems are held within the foliage.

Three specimens of *Phormium tenax* provide a core planting of energetic spears.

A reliable brown sedge, *Carex buchananii* reaches about 75cm (30in). For brighter colour, substitute *Uncinia rubra*.

This *Dianella nigra* offers good year-round form, with superb dark blue berries in autumn. *Libertia grandiflora* would make a good alternative.

Acaena is a ground-hugging ground-cover, here interplanted with the neat, blue-grey tussocks of *Poa colensoi*.

Podocarpus nivalis is a spreading conifer, elegantly cloud-pruned by nature. It grows to no more than 1m (3ft) high and contrasts most effectively with soaring and spiky plants.

Use *Libertia peregrinans* for its beautiful, gold colouring and spring flowers.

Cortaderia richardii is a handsome, early-flowering grass with arching leaves that have shiny undersides. The leaves reach up to 2cm (¾in) in width and 2m (6½ft) in length in its native habitat (but half that size in northern Europe). When flowering, it soars to nearly 3m (10ft), with long plumes of creamy buff, fading to white.

Planting list

1 New Zealand flax (*Phormium tenax*)

2 Toe toe (*Cortaderia richardii*)

3 Tussock grass (*Chionochloa flavescens*)

4 New Zealand red tussock grass (*Chionochloa rubra* subsp. *cuprea*)

5 Leatherleaf sedge (*Carex buchananii*)

6 New Zealand blueberry (*Dianella nigra*, syn. *D. intermedia*)

7 New Zealand iris (*Libertia peregrinans*)

8 *Muehlenbeckia astonii*

9 Mountain totara (*Podocarpus nivalis*)

10 Pirri-pirri bur (*Acaena inermis* 'Purpurea')

11 Blue shore tussock (*Poa colensoi*)

Project The All-Black container

This striking container offers maximum impact, using a backbone of New Zealand plants to create an easy-care year-round arrangement with undeniable panache. The key plant is the lancewood, with its extraordinary, spiky, black leaves.

You will need

Container

Crocks, old plant cells or broken polystyrene (Styrofoam)

Potting mix

Horticultural grit

Selection of plants: *Pseudopanax crassifolius*, *Leptospermum scoparium* 'Winter Cheer', dwarf *Hebe* 'Black Beauty', *Pittosporum tenuifolium* 'Tom Thumb', *Heuchera* 'Palace Purple', *Aeonium* 'Zwartkop'

Loam-based potting mix

Slow-release fertilizer granules

Decorative mulch

Aftercare

• These drought-tolerant specimens are forgiving if you forget them to water them from time to time.
• Occasional applications of slow-release fertilizer is all the feeding they need.
• Snip a few leaves off the heuchera if it threatens to overwhelm the shrubby planting.
• As long as you keep it on the dry side, this container will survive winter snow and lows of at least -12°C (10°F). It will last several years before the plants outgrow their space.

1 Choose a container. This black resin cube complements the edgy, modern planting, but still has some texture. Place it in its final position before you begin, as the container will be heavy to move once planted.

2 Immerse each plant in a bucket of water until the bubbles rise. Even drought-tolerant plants need a thorough soaking to get them off to a good start.

3 Put crocks in the base of the pot, or use old plant cells or pieces of broken polystyrene (plastic foam) if you prefer. Good drainage is essential for these plants.

4 Half fill with potting mix, to which you have added a few handfuls of horticultural grit. A deep pot like this can be part filled with home-made garden compost – even if there are a few annual weed seeds, they will be too deep to germinate.

5 Place the lancewood (*Pseudopanax crassifolius*) in a back corner of the pot. The planting will feed round in a spiral, from tallest to lowest, designed to be viewed from three sides, finishing with small ones that trail over the edge.

6 Add the remaining plants. Fill the gaps with a loam-based potting mix, along with some slow-release fertilizer. Although these are not hungry plants, they are tightly packed. Water and top with a decorative mulch.

The Cape garden

When the first director of the Royal Botanic Gardens at Kew engaged his very first plant collector in 1772, the destination they chose was South Africa. They were not disappointed: the sun-drenched shores of the Cape Peninsula proved a floral paradise. In just three years some of the most astonishing plants ever seen were collected: red hot pokers and African blue lilies, curious succulents and spectacular proteas, almost 50 different varieties of pelargonium and the dazzling bird of paradise flower.

Today the Cape Floral Kingdom is recognized as a World Heritage Site. No other country comes close to South Africa for the beauty, wealth and diversity of its flowers. Of the 22,500 species that grow there, some 16,500 grow nowhere else. And while a handful of these plants, such as *Zantedeschia*, *Streptocarpus*, gladioli and lobelia have become garden favourites, so vast and under-explored is this resource that we are only just beginning to appreciate its infinite possibilities. In the rapidly warming gardens of the northern hemisphere in particular, a ravishing new plant palette awaits.

Opposite
The South African garden at the Garden House in Devon shows how successfully these plants can adapt, growing on an elevated site in one of the wettest parts of Britain.

Above left
This is a hybrid between *Protea burchelli* and *Protea longifolia,* two of some 115 protea species in the Cape. It requires hot summers, full sun and a well-drained soil low in phosphates and nitrates.

Above right
The bird of paradise flower (*Strelitzia reginae*) is native to the tropical areas of South Africa and South America. It can be grown outdoors in a mild climate, but in more uncertain temperatures it should be kept in a greenhouse or brought indoors for the autumn and winter months.

The Cape climate and its flora

The astonishing diversity of plants in South Africa is the result of the unusual range of climates in the region. Travelling eastwards, the climate shifts from arid semi-desert to humid sub-tropical, with Mediterranean and alpine areas thrown in for good measure.

South Africa is sharply divided between areas receiving rain in winter and those receiving rain in summer, plus a few which enjoy moisture all year round. Different plants thrive in these different conditions, although a few adaptable species prosper in both. The winter-rainfall area of the Cape extends in an arc along the coast from the Orange River to Port Elizabeth, lying between the mountains and the sea. Rainfall is

heaviest near the coast, which enjoys a Mediterranean climate: hot in summer, wet and windy in winter, with just the occasional frost inland. The countryside consists of steep, rocky hills and wide valleys, with very poor, acidic, sandy soil. This supports a shrubby, drought-tolerant flora known as 'fynbos', named by early settlers after the 'fine-leaved bushes' which proved to be disappointing feed for pampered European cattle.

Among some 9,000 species, four main plant groups predominate. The most arresting are the proteas, leathery-leaved, shrubby plants ranging from 1–4m (3–13ft) high, of which many species are cultivated for cut flowers. Several species

Above left
Two of the main fynbos groups are the Cape heaths, with over 800 species, and the leucadenrons, members of the protea family. Here, *Erica diaphana* flowers among leucadendron hybrids.

Above right
Leucadendrons are often overlooked in favour of their showier relatives, the proteas and pincushion plants (*Leucospermum*), yet their superb foliage and shapely bracts make a fine contribution to the garden.

have aromatic leaves, which combine with the scented leaves of native pelargoniums to create the distinctive aroma of the fynbos. Warmer, drier summers may now allow gardeners in temperate climates to experiment with this magnificent plant group. At home in South Africa, Australia, New Zealand, Israel, Chile, Portugal, Hawaii and some parts of southern and northern California, many species of *Protea*, *Leucospermum* and *Leucadendron* also thrive as far north as south-west England and Ireland. Among the proteas grow colourful Cape heaths (*Erica* species), whose vivid blooms are as unlike our drab suburban heathers as it is possible to get; and some 300 species of *Restio*, graceful reed-like plants varying from 20cm (8in) to 3m (10ft) high, which make a fine alternative to grasses in the garden.

Often, especially in summer, the mountains of the Cape Peninsula are wreathed in cloud (known locally as the 'tablecloth on Table Mountain'),

providing year-round moisture for the last group, the corms and bulbs. Fynbos is the richest bulb region in the world, and in spring the hillsides are flushed with colourful drifts of *Watsonia*, *Gladiolus*, *Ornithogalum*, *Ixia*, and delicate freesia-like *Babiana*.

Here, too, the belladonna lily (*Amaryllis belladonna*) flowers after the heat of a long summer or, most brilliantly, after a fire. Fire plays a crucial role in the ecology of the fynbos, where plants can expect to be burned to the ground every 12 to 15 years. Fynbos plants have therefore evolved to renew themselves either from seed, as with the proteas and restios, or – less drastically – by resprouting from bulbs or rhizomes. This resilience offers a helpful safety net to gardeners in colder climates, where plants cut down by an unexpected chill will generally rise again. It does, however, make certain fynbos plants very difficult to propagate: the seeds of restio, for example, need to be treated with smoke in order to germinate.

Below left
This hybrid protea is a member of one of the most distinctive fynbos plant families. The family includes *Leucadendron* and *Leucospermum* species as well as *Protea*.

Below right
Sparaxis is a member of the iris family, easy to grow in Mediterranean climates. The fynbos is exceptionally rich in bulbous plants, which appear during the winter growing season.

The flowering desert

Further up the west coast and inland, the amount of rain diminishes rapidly. The Karoo, meaning 'dry place', is a high desert plateau and lower-lying arid region that is the home of many cacti and succulents, including the beautiful aloe family and some 600 species of *Mesembryanthemum*, known locally as 'Vygies'. These can make a spectacular contribution to the dry garden, able to withstand prolonged periods of drought.

To the west of the Cape lies Naquamaland, which every August and September puts on an extraordinary floral display. After the winter rains, the dusty valleys spring abruptly into life, flooded, seemingly overnight, with a sea of bulbs and a vast array of daisies – not only the annual 'Naquamaland daisies' (*Dimorphotheca sinuata*) and *Ursinisa speciosa* in orange, red and chrome-yellow, but bright-eyed *Osteospermum*, golden *Gazania*, scarlet and vermilion *Arctotis*, soft blue *Felicia* and sheets of vibrantly coloured succulents such as Livingstone daisies (*Dorotheanthus bellidiformis*) and tiny, waxy relatives of the sunflower, *Senecio serpens* and *S. talinoides*.

Many cultivars of these plants are sold worldwide for summer bedding, being very quick and easy to raise from seed. Though generally treated as annuals, *Osteospermum* and *Arctotis*, in particular, can now be kept through the winter, and *O. jucundum* is a popular permanent planting in temperate seaside gardens. The key to success with these, as with all fynbos plants, is drainage: although accustomed to winter rain, they will not sit in sodden soil (though *Arctotis* is remarkably tolerant). Overfeeding should be avoided. Although pelargoniums are glad to be indulged with copious feeding, most Cape plants react badly to nutrient-rich soils and fertilizers rich in phosphates, as their roots are adapted to survival in a mineral-starved habitat. If your ground is rich, they may fare better in a low-nutrient, gritty potting mix in a container.

Above left
Aloes, both large and small, make stunning garden plants. In this dry garden in Berkeley, California, *Aloe barberae* is set off by smaller aloes and fynbos plants such as Cape heaths and leucadendrons.

Above right
Flowering aloes and arctotis make a sumptuous display in an arid New Zealand rock garden.

Summer rain plants

From the summer rainfall areas of South Africa come some of the most beautiful garden plants. They include many that are familiar in colder climes as bedding plants and house plants, as well as stunning summer bulbs like agapanthus.

An explosion of colour

Many familiar bedding plants, such as *Diascia*, *Bacopa* and *Nemesia,* come from the southern part of the Highveld high grassland habitat in South Africa's eastern interior. Here, summers are warm and wet, with daily showers, and altitudes ranging from 1,000–3,000m (3,000–10,000ft), winter night can be severe, dropping as low as -15°C (5°F). On these grassy mountain slopes grow some of the most beautiful plants, including *Agapanthus*, *Dierama*, *Eucomis* and *Kniphofia*, elegant *Galtonia candicans* and dainty *Nerine bowdenii*. *Phygelius* grows in the clefts between rocks alongside fast-moving streams; *Crocosmia* and *Schizostylis coccinea* on riverbanks and in marshes. These summer rain plants will thrive anywhere with wet summers, including the United Kingdom and temperate parts of the USA.

On the coast, the 'Garden Route' east of the Cape is a sub-tropical area of year-round rain, and home to houseplants such as *Streptocarpus* and *Clivia*. Moving eastwards, habitat changes to summer-wet grassland, and evergreen agapanthus grows in abundance.

Left
Deciduous agapanthus (*A. campanulatus*, *A. inapertus*, *A. nutans* and *A. caulescens*) enjoy an open, sunny position with good drainage. Though generally hardy, protect the crown with a dry mulch if a prolonged cold snap is expected. The evergreens (*A. praecox* and *A. africanus*) are more tender, and will not tolerate winter wet. So in damp, temperate climates they are best grown in containers, and moved to a light, dry, frost-free shed or unheated glasshouse for the winter months.

Tutorial | Getting the best display from potted agapanthus

Agapanthus flower best in an open, sunny position. There is a widespread myth that they thrive on crowded roots and thin rations. Expert nurserymen, however, recommend regular feeding and ample pots. Flowering falls off visibly once a plant becomes too congested, and since agapanthus resent disturbance and generally refuse to flower the year after repotting or dividing, it is wise to give them as long as you can between these operations.

1 Feed fortnightly with a dilute balanced liquid feed during the growing season until the flowers begin to colour. Feed again when the flowers die down.

2 If flowering is poor, divide the plant the following spring. Ease the congested clump from the pot, cut it in half with a knife, and tease the roots apart.

3 Repot in a gritty loam-based potting compost, and keep well fed and watered. It will sulk for a season, but should flower with renewed vigour thereafter.

Right
Phygelius is a genus of fast-growing shrubs or sub-shrubs valued for their pendent trumpet-shaped flowers which bloom all summer long. There are two species, *Phygelius capensis* and *P. aequalis*.

Below
This colourful late summer planting with red hot pokers and agapanthus is the inspiration for the plan opposite.

Flowers of summer bulbs

It is curious that summer bulbs have not achieved the popularity of their spring cousins, when they are so desirable in many ways – inexpensive, easy to grow, and an invaluable source of summer colour. Just as a mid-summer display begins to wane, a handful of bulbs will add interest and variety, without taking up any additional space. These bulbs also look superb grown together. At the Garden House in Devon, southern England, a South African garden, originally inspired by the Naquamaland flowering desert, now features a

remarkable, naturalistic display of summer bulbs grown among *Phygelius*, poppies and evergreen grasses. Massing them together underlines their individual beauties: the intense, singing colour of crocosmias, the ethereal delicacy of dieramas and species gladioli, the exotic pineapple forms of eucomis, the blithe energy of red hot pokers, especially some of the more refined forms like *Kniphofia* 'Jenny Bloom'. The phygelius running between them provides a colourful, long-lasting background – but has to be chopped back ruthlessly every spring to keep it within bounds.

This informal style suggests another way of growing some of the larger bulbs, as a meadow planting among grasses. Robust, self-supporting, drought-tolerant and seemingly impervious to slugs and snails, they are well adapted to such plantings, which mirror their natural habitat.

Smaller varieties will need a little more care and attention. *Nerine bowdenii*, for example, needs a hot, dry position such as the base of a wall, where they can bake with their noses above the ground, whereas *Schizostylis* requires a sunny but moist position to flower freely.

Garden plan **A late summer border**

This selection of vigorous, easy-to-grow bulbs, interplanted with evergreen grass and phygelius, will give you colour from mid-summer until the first frosts, with fresh evergreen foliage and attractive seedheads extending the season of interest.

Tall and stately, with fiery red flowers and bright foliage, *Crocosmia* 'Lucifer' is handsome in bud, and the spent flower spike is striking many weeks after flowering.

Dierama 'Buckland White' is a sturdy white hybrid that makes a good alternative to the more common pink varieties. It provides a strong architectural statement in the border, long after flowering.

The orange-tawny flowers of *Kniphofia* 'Tawny King' open from brown buds on tall (1.2m/4ft) bronze stems.

A stunning new long-flowering hybrid, *Agapanthus* 'Jacks Blue' bears large heads of intense purple-blue flowers on tall stems (1.2–1.5m/4–5ft) through the summer.

The lime-green pineapple flowers of *Eucomis bicolor*, are edged in purple, with attractive mottled stems.

Kniphofia 'Bees Lemon' is a small (85cm/3ft) and ladylike poker with lemon blooms opening from green buds, and relatively neat evergreen foliage.

Following on from 'Navy Blue', the lovely pale blue *Agapanthus* 'Angela' is a good vigorous cultivar despite its delicate, slightly droopy looks.

Crocosmia 'Debutante' is a dainty small (60cm/24in) montbretia with a soft orange flower and fine foliage.

Agapanthus 'Navy Blue' is a really dark blue, of medium size (80cm/2½ft), flowering mid-season.

Chionochloa rubra, or New Zealand red tussock grass, gives colour and structure through the year before the bulbs come into their own.

Dark bronzy foliage sets off the bright apricot flowers of *Crocosmia* x *crocosmiiflora* 'Coleton Fishacre'.

Planting list

1 *Agapanthus* 'Jacks Blue'
2 *Agapanthus* 'Navy Blue'
3 *Agapanthus* 'Angela'
4 New Zealand red tussock grass (*Chionochloa rubra*)
5 Montbretia (*Crocosmia* x *crocosmiiflora* 'Coleton Fishacre')
6 Montbretia (*Crocosmia* 'Debutante')
7 Montbretia (*Crocosmia* 'Lucifer')
8 Angel's fishing rod (*Dierama* 'Buckland White')
9 Pineapple lily (*Eucomis bicolor*)
10 Red hot poker (*Kniphofia* 'Bees Lemon')
11 Red hot poker (*Kniphofia* 'Tawny King')
12 Phygelius (*Phygelius* x *rectus* 'Somerford Funfair' series)

Plant focus Flowers for late summer colour

Keep your garden full of colour until the very end of the summer with a planting of these vibrant late-flowering South African beauties, most of which are extremely easy to grow. (See also page 151.)

Crocosmia 'Lucifer'

Crocosmia Montbretia

The botanical name is derived from the scent of the flowers, which are supposed to smell like saffron crocuses, but these handsome plants are also commonly known in many parts of the world as montbretia. The species *Crocosmia* that grow along gullies and riverbanks in South Africa have been much improved by plant breeders to offer gardeners a magnificent array of joyously coloured plants for the late summer garden. The large cultivar 'Lucifer' is deservedly popular, being tall and strong-growing, with luminous, pillar-box red blooms and neat fans of bright green leaves. Almost as vigorous, but rather more dainty, is 'Emily Mackenzie', with large, long-lasting, dark orange flowers with a distinctive pale eye. 'Jenny Bloom' is even more ladylike, with yellow flowers held in elegant curving sprays above pleated leaves. Several cultivars are available with dark, bronzy foliage, such as *C. x crocosmiiflora* 'Coleton Fishacre' and *C. x c.* 'Dusky Maiden' – these do better with a little shade. Montbretias dislike dry, dusty soil and cold wet clay, but a happy plant in rich soil, with plenty of summer moisture, will romp away and probably need dividing every third year. Grow it anyway – like eucomis, it is a fabulous plant for a hot jungle border.

Eucomis 'John Huxtable'

Eucomis comosa

Crocosmia 'Jenny Bloom'

Eucomis Pineapple flower, pineapple lily

With its pineapple flower and lush, tropical leaves, eucomis looks wildly exotic, but is actually very easy to grow. This is the one for gardeners who cannot offer perfect drainage, since its natural habitat is the riverbank, and it likes a drop of moisture. Eucomis is hardy, and will even benefit from a frost, which helps the bulb to split so that more flower spikes are produced the following year. Eucomis range in size from dainty *E. vandermerwei*, just 8cm (3in) high, to *E. pole-evansii*, which tops 1.8m (6ft). *E. v.* 'Octopus' is a new and very attractive hybrid form of the tiny rare species, with dark green foliage flecked with maroon, resembling, as its name suggests, a small cephalopod. Another striking maroon is *E. comosa* 'Sparkling Burgundy' (60cm/2ft), with glossy leaves and wine-coloured flowers. Its green-flowered parent, *E. comosa*, is widely available, and equally handsome, as is two-toned *E. bicolor*. Graceful *E.* 'John Huxtable' is another beauty with large, loose, starry flowers. For a taller variety, try *E. autumnalis* subsp. *autumnalis* 'Peace Candles', a glowing white with very sturdy, wind-proof stems.

Eucomis bicolor

Watsonia Bugle lily

Similar to gladioli, watsonias deserve to be far more widely grown. Given a warm, sunny, sheltered site in good, well-drained soil, they will reward you with a profusion of delicate flower-spikes in shades of red, pink and orange. The Tresco hybrids, with grassy evergreen foliage, a remarkably long flowering period, and a colour range encompassing lilacs and purples, are perhaps the first choice for the gardener. Size varies from 60–120cm (2–4ft). Among named varieties, *W. angusta* bears spikes of scarlet flowers on stems up to 60cm (2ft), while *W. meriana* has outsize pinky-orange blooms. *W. pillansii* is sturdy and easy, with tall (90cm/3ft) stems of brilliant orange flowers, and *W. borbonica* is a beautiful giant from the southern Cape, growing to 1.5m (5ft), with large pink flowers. All benefit from a dry winter mulch.

Watsonia 'Tresco Dwarf Pink'

Schizostylis coccinea

Kniphofia 'Jenny Bloom'

Kniphofia Red hot poker

Also known as torch lilies, these plants are well named for their stiff, upright stems, shooting from a basal rosette of strappy, evergreen leaves. The spires of brightly coloured, tubular flowers open over a long period, starting from the bottom, the buds often of a different colour from the open flower, giving the pokers their distinctive two-tone appearance. As well as all the fiery shades, there are pale green and cream pokers, but what is the point of a poker that does not burn? Statures range from the splendid *K. uvaria* 'Nobilis', with 2.4m (8ft) spikes of orange-red, to knee-high *K.* 'Little Maid', best planted in drifts. *K.* 'Jenny Bloom' is a particularly lovely variety, with a loosely formed spike of soft apricot flowers. *K. caulescens* is a handsome, woody-stemmed variety with unusual blue foliage. While pokers need summer moisture to thrive, they also need good winter drainage. On heavier ground, dig in plenty of grit and organic matter, and give the crowns winter protection to stop them rotting.

Nerine

Flowering from late summer into autumn, nerines offer a last delicious blast of summer colour. The most glamorous are the varieties of Guernsey lily (*N. sarniensis*), in shades of orange, scarlet and purple, with a delicate glitter to the petals, as if brushed with stardust. But these really need glasshouse cultivation. For the garden, choose *N. bowdenii*, with bright-pink flowers clustered at the top of leafless stems. To thrive, the bulbs need to be shallow planted in the hottest, driest place you can find, and, once established, will grow into large colonies. They flower best when congested. The leaves follow the flower in winter, then the plant goes dormant in summer when it needs a good baking. Many gorgeous, girly shades are available: *N.* 'Purple Stripe' is shocking pink, with a shimmering centre and a seam of purple up the centre of each reflexed petal. More sedate, but strong-growing, is *N.* 'Albivetta', in a very pale pink.

Schizostylis Kaffir lily

Spikes of blossom about 45cm (18in) tall are borne in late summer and autumn above narrow sword-shaped evergreen leaves. All schizostylis derive from red-flowered *S. coccinea*, but modern cultivars have much larger blooms and a wide range of colours, including whites (*S. c.* 'Pallida'), purples, corals and salmon (*S. c.* 'Jennifer'). Clear pink, strong-growing *S. c.* 'Vicountess Byng' is a deservedly popular variety, and will flower all winter if not cut down by frost. Bulbs are frost-hardy. It looks excellent paired with a small, colourful grass such as *Festuca glauca* or *Uncinia rubra*. Schizostylis need lots of moisture, and, very usefully, will even grow in waterlogged ground.

Nerine bowdenii

Project Making a daisy chair

Gazanias, the jolliest of South African daisies, flower from early summer right through to the first frosts with large starry flowers in a riot of hot shades that open wide in the sun. Set them off with a brilliant blue paint that recalls a sunny Cape sky.

You will need

An old dining chair, ideally one where the seat lifts out

Sandpaper

Exterior undercoat or a combination of matt varnish and emulsion

Hessian (burlap) to line the chair

Hammer and tacks

Black plastic

A selection of young gazanias – plug plants are ideal. Alternatively you could use other daisy flowers such as *Arctosis* or smaller varieties of *Osteospermum*.

Lightweight potting mix

Gravel for top dressing

Care of gazanias

• Gazanias are short-lived, half-hardy perennials, usually treated as annuals in cooler climates. They are easy to grow, but need protection from excessively wet or frosty conditions.
• Regular dead-heading will keep the flowers coming until temperatures start to drop.
• Gazanias are usually sold as colour mixtures, as seeds or as young plants which you can grow on. Pinch out the plants to keep them compact.

1 Choose a good, strong, heavy wooden chair that won't blow over in the wind, remove the seat, then sand it down carefully to remove all the old varnish.

2 Paint with a flat oil-based paint such as an exterior undercoat, or, if using emulsion, give it a good thick coat of matt varnish. Unprotected emulsion will go mouldy when it gets wet.

3 Cut out a square of hessian (burlap) to make a base for the planting. An old peanut sack will do very well. Tack it firmly into the base of the chair and trim away any excess.

4 Line with a square of perforated black plastic to stop the water draining through quite so fast. The broad, shallow planting area will dry out very quickly, rather like a hanging basket.

5 It is best to choose young plants to fill this very shallow planting area (remember their soil is shallow and poor in the wild). Pack them in and fill round with a lightweight peat-substitute potting mix containing a little water-retaining gel.

6 Top dress with a layer of gravel, then move to the greenhouse to let the planting fill out, just as you would with a hanging basket. When all danger of frosts is past set the chair outside in your warmest and sunniest spot.

The jungle garden

'Jungle' plants may come from a huge range of habitats, from coral island to cloud forest, but generally share a need for heat and humidity. But rising average temperatures mean that many of these plants, particularly the hardier specimens from higher altitudes, can now be grown outdoors in cooler latitudes, at least for the summer months.

Translated into other climate zones, the jungle garden works best in isolation – a horticultural conjuring trick that can transform a city yard into a stand of verdant rainforest, a familiar garden into an intoxicating tropical oasis. Instead of the fleeting charms of cottage-garden plants, here are flowers that bloom for months on end, heady scents and brazen colours. Here are leaves the size of surf-boards, and improbable plants that grow into giants from seed in a matter of weeks.

The jungle garden is alluring precisely because it is a fantasy – an escape into a private dreamworld. Best of all, it is a dream that can flourish in the most unpromising locations, turning overlooked urban backyards and dank, shaded spaces into islands of sun-drenched tropical enchantment.

The lure of the jungle

Tropical plants have captivated gardeners for centuries. The astonishing plants brought back by the plant hunters to temperate climes could at first be enjoyed only by the super-rich, cosseted in costly stove-houses. But by the mid-19th century, any well-to-do family could aspire to a conservatory stocked with orchids and pitcher plants, palms and bromeliads, and all kinds of colourful exotica.

In Germany, Paris and London, the new public parks brought these dazzling, unfamiliar plants to a wider audience. By 1864, London's Battersea Park was using the same plants as today's most 'cutting-edge' garden designers – tree ferns and bananas, cannas and palms, yuccas and phormiums, placing them among low-growing plants or singly in grass.

All that changed with the advent of World War I – once fuel and labour were no longer cheap, exotics were too expensive to maintain. But from the 1960s, as cheap air travel allowed more people to travel further afield, a new style of jungle gardening began to emerge – one based less on plant collecting than using a blend of tender and hardy plants to create a distant tropical paradise. As temperatures steadily rise in temperate zones, many more gardeners are experimenting with tropicals outside the greenhouse, rejoicing in their thrilling colour and lush, oversized foliage.

A jungle garden should be a place of wonder and joy: an imaginative and sensory as well as horticultural adventure. Most of us in temperate climes will be testing the limits of hardiness of our plants. We won't always get it right, and must expect a few casualties along the way. We will also make discoveries – plants do not always behave as described in books. The important thing is to be bold!

Above left
In a sleepy English village, a lepidopterist has created a garden that recalls his butterfly-hunting expeditions in the jungle.

Above right
The hot selection of tropical plants in this garden include *Dahlia* 'Bishop of Llandaff'.

Opposite
The New Zealand black tree fern *Cyathea medullaris* is among the most graceful and evocative of jungle plants.

Planning your jungle

Exotic jungle plants are a wonderful way to breathe life and drama into small, sheltered town gardens. Fortunately locations that are short of light and enclosed by surrounding walls make absolutely perfect sites for these specimens.

Getting started

The ideal location for a jungle garden is a warm, sheltered spot out of the wind – the microclimates of town gardens offer optimum conditions. On a more exposed site you will need protective screening (this should not be solid, but 50 per cent permeable to the wind). Most gardens have both sunny and shady areas, and there are suitable plants for both situations, as well as many that will like to shelter under the canopy of jungle giants. Sufficient moisture is vital: many exotics such as tree ferns and cannas grow naturally in very humid conditions, while aroids and bananas grow in direct proportion to the amount of food and water you give them. Finally, decide how much work you are willing to put in. Are you prepared to rush outside with your fleece every time a frost is forecast, or would you prefer trouble-free plants that just look exotic? In many temperate zones, such as the more southerly parts of Britain and the USA, plants such as dahlias and cannas, once routinely lifted, can now be left in the ground through the winter. But if you are tempted by some of the luscious tender or half hardy plants that must have winter protection, then you will need a frost-free shed or greenhouse.

Below left
This British garden combines Tasmanian tree fern *Dicksonia antarctica*, which needs winter protection, with the horse chestnut leaves of *Rodgersia aesculifolia*, which is completely hardy.

Below right
Palms, bamboos, bananas and decking make an exciting and low-maintenance alternative to conventional lawn and flower borders in this narrow town garden.

Opposite
Trachycarpus fortunei dominates a small but atmospheric London garden.

Creating a framework

The jungle garden is at its best from summer through to the first frosts, so to avoid spending winters looking at bare earth, a backbone of all-year-round planting is essential. The obvious starting point is a framework of evergreens – hardy palms such as the Chusan palm (*Trachycarpus fortunei*) or the European fan palm (*Chamaerops humilis*), phormiums or cordylines, *Magnolia grandiflora* or *Fatsia japonica* – all plants that hit the right exotic note, but are reliably hardy. Bamboos are also invaluable, both for structure and for screening, but be aware of their assertive habits! The fargesias, such as *Fargesia rufa*, are the ones to go for in a small garden. Smaller plants such as the lovely dappled *Arum italicum* subsp. *italicum* 'Marmoratum' can also contribute valuable winter interest, as can the skeletons of deciduous shrubs and trees selected for their dramatic foliage potential.

Tutorial | Pruning bamboo

Keep established bamboos neat and colourful with regular grooming. Many of the smaller bamboos can be pruned back to the ground in spring to encourage fresh, new growth – the emerging culms will be much more strongly variegated than the old. Bamboos such as *Phyllostachys* also benefit from tidying the culms. Do not clear away fallen leaves, but let them compost down around the plant to replace valuable silica, which is essential for strong growth. Bamboos are greedy feeders, so a good mulch of manure or garden compost will also be appreciated.

1 Remove any weak and spindly culms, and cut away any that are crowding each other, so you are left with strong, well-spaced growth. Make your cuts flush to the ground. You may need loppers to remove fatter culms.

2 Using secateurs (pruners), trim away the lateral growth at the bottom third of the plant (about 1.2m/4ft). This will reveal the culms in all their glory, and give the plant a neater, more architectural look.

3 You can remove up to a third of the culms, cutting out from the centre as well as the edge of the clump to achieve a see-through effect. The more you cut out, the fatter and showier the remaining culms will become.

Large-leaved majesty

Oversized leaves in contrasting shapes and textures are the very essence of the jungle garden. Go for a happy hurly-burly of different leaf forms, packing them in at every level for a satisfyingly lush and luxurious effect.

Jungle leaf choices

For superb architectural form, there is nothing to match the tree ferns, while the great flapping leaves of bananas offer an instant ticket to the Tropics, especially underplanted with equally flamboyant colocasias. These are aroids, a family that includes elephant's ear (*Alocasia*), arum lilies (*Zantedeschia*) and the Swiss cheese plant (*Monstera deliciosa*), all excellent summer additions to the garden. Moisture-loving *Colocasia esculenta* offers many showy varieties with large, pointed leaves and dramatic veining: *C. e.* 'Nancyana' is streaked with yellow, *C. e.* 'Fontanesii' has a purply tinge, while *C. e.* 'Black Magic' is a show-stopping matt black.

On a warmer, drier site, try some palms – there are over 100 species that will survive outside, even in the gloomy British Isles. The more mature the palm, the more resilient it will be, so grow palms on in pots for the first few years, before planting them permanently. Provide perfect winter drainage and protection from cold, drying winds. The jelly palm (*Butia capitata*) and Mexican blue palm (*Brahea armata*) both grow well in pots, as does a fine, blue version of the fan palm, *Chamaerops humilis* var. 'Cerifera' (also sold as 'Argentea').

Big-leaved climbers such as *Actinidia deliciosa, Aristolochia macrophylla* or *Vitis coignetiae* will also contribute to the atmosphere, as does fast-growing *Ricinus communis* and the inimitable rice paper plant, *Tetrapanax papyrifer*. Equally impressive is the primeval giant *Gunnera manicata*, which works well with monster grasses such as *Miscanthus sacchariflorus* or the giant reed, *Arundo donax*, but only if you have plenty of room to spare!

Pruning for outsize foliage

There are certain trees and shrubs that will produce enormous, tropical-looking leaves if you prune them very hard in the spring. Left to its own devices, the foxglove tree (*Paulownia tomentosa*) will make a handsome, round-topped tree with racemes of purple flowers, but if you prune it to one bud above the ground in spring, each stem can grow up to 3m (10ft) long in one season, producing leaves up to 50cm (20in) across; the fewer the stems, the bigger the foliage. The Indian bean tree (*Catalpa bignonioides*) can be treated in a similar fashion, producing vast, heart-shaped, pale green leaves. Even workaday shrubs like *Cotinus* and elder (*Sambucus*) can produce fabulous foliage effects if hard-pruned in this way, notably red-leaved *Cotinus* 'Grace' and golden *Sambucus* 'Plumosa Aurea'.

Below
Colocasia esculenta, including this 'Black Magic' cultivar, is most widely grown as a food plant, but there are also many fine ornamental varieties, such as *C. e.* 'Illustris', *C. e.* 'Mojito' or *C. e.* 'Wild Taro'.

Plant focus Tree ferns and bananas

The statuesque forms of tree ferns and bananas bring an instant air of the exotic to the garden. They will happily survive in a temperate climate given winter care and will amply repay the effort required (see also page 134).

Tree ferns

Though popular as single specimens, tree ferns look most magical when planted in groves (even a group of three) and underplanted with other ferns. Tasmanian *Dicksonia antarctica* is the most reliable and widely available variety; while more delicate *D. squarrosa* and the hardiest of the New Zealand varieties, *Cyathea dealbata*, are well worth the trouble of giving them winter protection. Although *D. antarctica* will grow in full sun if watered daily, it really needs a damp, shady, sheltered spot and a rich acid soil to thrive. The 'trunk' is an above-ground root system, needing to be kept moist at all times, by watering into the centre of the trunk and allowing the water to run down it. (A drip irrigation system fixed to the plant is ideal.) In these conditions, new fronds will uncurl from the central growing point in just a few weeks. The plant as a whole, though, is very slow-growing, putting on no more than 30cm (12in) in 10 years. That is why they are so expensive! (See also page 153.)

Dicksonia antarctica

Ensete ventricosum 'Maurelii'

Bananas

Often described as 'trees', bananas are, in fact, colossal herbs. The 'trunk' is not woody, but is made up of tightly wrapped leaf bases (botanically, a 'pseudostem'). The huge, arching leaves are prone to shred – an adaptation to stop them being torn off during tropical storms. So to enjoy their full beauty, place them out of the wind, where they can be back-lit by the low evening sun: the great, glowing paddles of semi-transparent green are stupendous. There are two principal genera: *Musa* (which includes the edible bananas) and *Ensete*. The clump-forming musas tend to be more umbrella-shaped, with leaves arching from the top, while the ensetes are more upright, with leaves growing up from a bulbous base. All respond to plenty of food and water. Kick-start them into growth with a generous feed and mulching in spring.

The Japanese banana (*Musa basjoo*), actually from China, is the toughest outdoor banana, reaching 2–3m (6½–10ft) in height, with mid-green leaves reaching 1.8m (6ft) long. The stem will be hardy to -10°C (14°F) if protected, and will reshoot if killed off by frost. For a smaller garden, or container, try equally hardy *Musa lasiocarpa*, which forms a dense clump of thick, blue-green leaves, only 1.2m (4ft) high, and bears curious, ochre-yellow flowerheads. At the other end of the scale is towering *Ensete ventricosum*, which produces bright green, paddle-like leaves up to 3m (10ft) long. Even more impressive is *E. v.* 'Maurelii', with red midribs and leaves suffused with purple. Both are tender, and must be overwintered at 5°C (41°F) – so some drastic hacking may be required!

Musa basjoo

Musa lasiocarpa

Tropical colours

A jungle garden is the perfect excuse to throw caution to the winds and go for the brightest, boldest colour combinations you dare, remembering that foliage can be even more dazzling than flowers.

Glamorous leaves

Some of the most dazzling colour effects in the garden are to be had from foliage. Shrubby evergreen *Solenostemon scutellarioides*, commonly known as coleus or flame nettle, has been a favourite bedding plant since Victorian times. Fast-growing, cheap, and available in every conceivable colour combination, it's an easy, if not exactly subtle, way to bring a zing to your colour scheme.

Every bit as vibrant are the cannas, which range from knee-high to banana-high, with large, broad leaves in myriad shades of purple, bronze and emerald. Many are magnificently patterned: *Canna* 'Pretoria' has startling green and golden stripes, while *C.* 'Durban' flaunts a psychedelic combination of purple, orange and pink. The orchid-shaped flowers are no less flamboyant: generally red, orange, salmon or yellow, some (like *C.* 'Picasso' or *C.* 'En Avant') extravagantly spotted, and all strong and long-lasting. The bulk of cannas is well set off by

equally bright but lighter-textured plants: airy *Verbena bonariensis*, abutilons, bright orange *Tithonia rotundifolia* 'Torch', or *Cleome hassleriana*, a spiky annual that can be grown from seed.

Cannas are very greedy plants, which tend to do well on heavy clay soils; there are even some types (the water cannas) that can be grown as pond marginals. Traditionally, once the stem is cut down by frost, cannas are lifted and the tubers stored in potting mix, sand or straw over winter. But if your soil is free-draining and your winters mild, try leaving them in place, with just a thick coat of mulch.

Flamboyant flowers

Closely related to the cannas are *Strelizia reginae*, the bird of paradise flower, and the gingers. These are outstanding plants, with fine foliage and long-lasting flowers. The ginger lilies (*Hedychium*) are the most widely grown for their showy, strongly scented flower-spikes. (*H. coccineum* 'Tara' is one

Right
Dahlias, such as this 'Nargold' cultivar, are ideal flowers for the jungle garden – large, bright and long-lasting.

Far right
No flowers are needed in this New Zealand jungle garden, where sub-tropical foliage plants provide a brilliant display.

Far left
Fascicularia bicolor has central leaves in a rich crimson and, when in bloom, distinctive sky-blue flowers.

Left centre
Variously known as 'Durban', 'Phasion' and 'Tropicanna', this variety has the most fabulously striped foliage of all the cannas.

Left
Clivia is just one of many familiar houseplants which originate in the tropics, and which look marvellous returned to their 'natural' jungle habitat. *Coleus*, *Caladium*, *Peperomia* and the large begonias will all grow more lustily outside, and when nights begin to cool, they can just be lifted and brought back indoors.

of the best forms.) Like cannas, they prefer a moist but free-draining, humus-rich soil, and will repay generous feeding and watering. But, unlike the sun-loving cannas, many gingers are forest-floor plants that thrive in shade. The dainty, orchid-flowered roscoeas are particularly lovely and, being fully hardy, deserve a place in any woodland garden.

Last but not least are two garden divas without which no tropical border would be complete. There are now over 44,000 cultivars of dahlia, so one of them is bound to appeal. (Treat them like cannas, and interplant with *Verbena bonariensis*, so you do not have to stake them.) Finally there are the brugmansias, with their outlandishly huge, dangling 'angel's trumpet' flowers. Plants like these are the gardener's friend – fast-growing, fabulously showy, and forgiving. They even smell exotic! Dig them up at the end of the season, reduce both stems and roots to a manageable size, store them in a plastic bag in the shed, and replant in spring. They will be romping away in no time. Do not be tempted to investigate brugmansia's hallucinogenic properties – every part of the plant is poisonous. Besides, you have a jungle garden to transport you from the dull everyday world into multi-coloured paradise!

Overwintering exotics

Tropical plants like hot and humid conditions. While higher average temperatures allow them to survive comfortably in a sheltered location in colder climates during the summer, they will need extra care during cold spells to survive.

Overwintering under cover

When the first frosts are forecast, it's time to dig up your tropical plants. Most jungle gardeners grow their more tender plants in pots, which can be sunk into the border for the summer, then easily lifted. Smaller palms and succulents will need a frost-free greenhouse or shed (they don't mind lack of light while dormant), sparmannia and tender salvias need to overwinter at a minimum of 5°C (41°F), so require a heated greenhouse, while houseplants that have enjoyed a season out of doors, such as philodendron, schefflera or Swiss cheese plants, will need to come back inside. The simplest way to overwinter aroids such as alocasias, colocasias or caladiums is to bring them indoors. Alternatively, once frost has blackened the leaves, you can lift and dry the tubers. Place the tubers in a box of sand and tuck them in the airing cupboard or under the bed. Replant in spring, water lightly, and put them in the bathroom to start into growth. Once under way, cut back the initial growth to the ground and allow to resprout. Acclimatize to lower temperatures gradually, and place back outside when the nights are suitably mild.

Overwintering in place

Larger plants that can't be moved will need protection in situ. Even if leaves are frost-damaged, as long as the growing point is safe, the plant will survive. So tie up the leaves of phormiums and cordylines into a protective bundle round the growing point, and mulch the crowns of perennials like *Tetrapanax* with a layer of grit to inhibit rotting, then a thick, light mulch, like bracken, that won't become too soggy. For *Gunnera manicata*, cut off the giant leaves and fold them over the crown, and for *Dicksonia antarctica*, stuff the crown with a handful of straw to protect the vulnerable new fronds as they emerge. Never use bubble-wrap – tree ferns must stay moist at all times. If prolonged frost is expected, wrap the top 30cm (12in) of the trunk with horticultural fleece, tying in place with some twine. Just remove frost-burned tips before unwrapping it again in spring.

Tutorial | Overwintering bananas

Your banana is more likely to die from winter wet than winter cold – the secret is to keep it dry and well ventilated.

Many books will tell you to wrap your banana in straw, or even to bury it in pine needles. But these materials will absorb moisture from the ground, enveloping the stalk in a soggy blanket and causing it to rot. This method is simple and tidy, and effective down to temperatures of -15°C (5°F).

1 Trim away all the dead foliage using a pruning saw, secateurs or sharp loppers.

2 Then cut down each banana stalk to a manageable height.

3 Select a length of wide, plastic drainage pipe and place it over your banana. Put a pierced lid over the pipe, such as a large flowerpot with a drainage hole.

Garden plan A colourful subtropical border

This border crams together a riotous selection of the plants highlighted in this chapter to create a hot, tropical effect. A framework of permanent planting is provided by bamboo, fatsia, paulownia, arums, and hardy bananas. The rest of the planting can be set out in late spring, and will put on a dazzling display of giant foliage and vibrant colour until the first frosts.

With strident reds, oranges and magentas, and much of the foliage in tones of bronze, purple and brown, this is not a border for the faint-hearted! Green-leaved varieties of ricinus, canna and dahlia could be used for a quieter effect, along with white rather than pink cleome, and the lime-green tobacco plant *Nicotiana langsdorfii* rather than lobelia and zinnia.

Ricinus communis 'Carmencita', with its massive, bronzy leaves, gives height and presence at the back of the border.

Fargesia rufa is a well-behaved bamboo that won't take over and will provide structure through the winter.

This wantonly exotic morning glory grows up a wigwam to bring some flower power to the back of the border.

Hedychium coccineum 'Tara' offers both scented, orange flowers and handsome, blue-green leaves.

The crimson stems and young shoots of *Ricinus communis* 'Impala' look well with the red of the banana behind it and contrast with the softer-textured paulownia.

Cleome can be grown from seed at minimal cost.

Choose a green variety of colocasia with an attractive leaf pattern.

The wild, spidery petals of *Zinnia* 'Red Spider' in a startling red will show to good effect against the glossy evergreen leaves of the structural *Fatsia* behind.

Planting list

1 Red-leaved banana (*Ensete ventricosum* 'Maurelii')

2 Castor oil plant (*Ricinus communis* 'Carmencita')

3 Bamboo (*Fargesia rufa*)

4 Morning glory (*Ipomoea purpurea* 'Star of Yalta')

5 Green-leaved banana (*Musa basjoo*)

6 Ginger lily (*Hedychium coccineum* 'Tara')

7 False castor oil plant (*Fatsia japonica*)

8 *Zinnia* 'Red Spider'

9 Elephant's ear (*Colocasia*)

10 *Dahlia* 'Bishop of Llandaff'

11 Lords and ladies (*Arum italicum* subsp. *italicum* 'Marmoratum')

12 *Dahlia* 'Dark Desire'

13 *Cleome hassleriana* 'Cherry Queen'

14 Indian shot plant (*Canna* 'Pretoria')

15 Foxglove tree (*Paulownia tomentosa*)

16 Castor oil plant (*Ricinus communis* 'Impala')

17 Chinese bellflower (variegated *Abutilon* 'Cannington Carol')

18 Indian shot plant (*Canna* 'Durban')

Project One-year wonders

Sowing from seed is easy and satisfying, especially with *Ricinus communis*, the castor oil plant. These amazing annuals reach huge sizes in a single season, growing (almost) before your very eyes. Use them as dramatic fillers between more permanent planting.

You will need

Ricinus communis seeds (here we use 'Carmencita')

Fresh potting mix

7.5cm (3in) pots, for initial sowing

Dibber

Gravel

Heated propagator or a warm shaded windowsill

Copper barrier or slug pellets for slug protection

Planting options

• *Ricinus communis* 'Carmencita' grows 2–3m (7–10ft) tall, with shiny mahogany foliage setting off red flower buds and gorgeous spiky seed heads.
• Smaller *R. c.* 'Impala' grows just 1.5–1.8m (5–6ft), with bronze-green leaves carried on red stems. Clusters of creamy-yellow flowers are followed by spectacular spikes of scarlet fruits.
• Use ricinus to add height and bulk to the jungle border.
• Planting in groups of three or more makes a spectacular thicket, ideal for screening.
• Place the seeds into humus-rich, free-draining soil in full sun.

1 Sow your chosen seeds (see options below left) in early spring. The seeds are beautiful, but very toxic. Ricinus is the source of the poison ricin – so keep the seeds away from children and do not eat any part of them.

2 Scarifying them with a file, or soaking them in water for 24 hours, will improve the rate of germination. When planting, use fresh potting mix, clean pots and a clean dibber – good hygiene is the enemy of fungal diseases.

3 Sow the seeds singly in small pots to a depth of 6mm (¼in) and water well.

4 Mulch each of the pots lightly with gravel to provide an insulating layer. Keep the pots well watered.

5 The optimum temperature for germination is 20–25ºC (70–75ºF), so for best results use a heated propagator. But you should still get over 50 per cent success if the pots are sited on a shaded windowsill in a heated room.

6 The first arched stems appear within ten days and grow to a stout 15cm (6in) seeding by the following week. Keep well fed and watered, and harden off by degrees, before planting out when all risk of frost has passed. Protect from slugs.

Plant directory

It is time to begin the experiment and discover what will grow in our rapidly changing gardens. The lists that follow are intended simply as starting points, and include both familiar and less familiar plants. But do bear in mind that no description can be a substitute for seeing a plant in real life, and talking to somebody who grows it. While the lists relate to specific chapters, there is inevitably much overlap, so we try to refer to both the origins of plants and how they might be useful in the garden.

USDA hardiness zones and RHS hardiness classifications are provided, but these can be no more than a rudimentary guide. Two gardens may be only yards apart, yet have totally different microclimates – and it is these that will ultimately determine the success or failure of a plant. Where does sun and shadow fall? Is there shelter from the wind? Is there a hot spot? Is there a spring, or something beneath the soil that affects the drainage? Questions like these will decide what will grow in your garden, and your most reliable guide will always be the evidence of your own eyes.

Opposite
Clouds of *Leucanthemum* and a sprinkling of *Osteospermum* swirl round spikes of echium and aloe on this bank of Mediterranean-style planting

Above left
Eryngium bourgatii 'Picos Blue' is an attractive specimen with blue-silver flowers and foliage. It loves a warm spot in full sun.

Above right
Passiflora caerulea (blue passionflower) is a vigorous climber for a sunny wall. The passionflower is evergreen in tropical climates, but drops its leaves where temperatures are cold in the winter.

Laurus nobilis

Myrtus communis subsp.
tarentina

Drought-tolerant shrubs for evergreen hedges and topiary

Almost any densely growing, small-leaved shrub can be clipped into a hedge or topiary form, from yew, santolina and rosemary to African boxwood (*Myrsine africana*) or *Leptospermum scoparium*. Those below are reliable and robust, and all prefer a well-drained site.

Buxus sempervirens
COMMON BOX

Vigorous, densely growing and tolerant of clipping, box is the most versatile of topiary plants, with varieties suitable for the tallest hedge as well as the most intricate knot or form. Inspect plants for the fungal disease box blight before buying. (See also pages 20, 22).
Height and **spread** 5m (15ft) (*B. s.*); 20cm (8in) (*B. s.* 'Suffruticosa'); 1m (3ft) x 1.5m (5ft) (*B. microphylla*)
Hardiness Hardy Z7–11

Cupressus sempervirens
ITALIAN CYPRESS

A slender tree characteristic of the Italian garden. (See also page 20.)
Height 10–15m (30–50ft)
Hardiness Frost hardy Z9–11

Laurus nobilis
BAY LAUREL, SWEET BAY

To the Greeks and Romans, bay was a symbol of wisdom and glory. There was no honour greater than a crown of its shiny, ovate, aromatic leaves. It will take shade in its Mediterranean homeland, but prefers a sunnier site in cooler climes. Fluffy yellow flowers are clustered along the branches in spring, followed by small black berries. It can grow into a large tree, but, seeming to thrive on clipping and constraint, it is ideal for potted topiary. *L. n. angustifolia* makes a marvellous hedge, with its narrower, willow-like leaves. The golden bay, *L. n.* 'Aurea', is apt to scorch, and is best avoided.
Height 9m (30ft); **spread** 6m (20ft)
Hardiness Frost hardy Z9–11

Myrtus communis
COMMON MYRTLE

This large shrub has been grown in gardens since ancient times and is valued for its neat, oval, dark green leaves. Dedicated to the goddess Venus, it was grown around her temples, and Venus is often shown rising from the sea carrying a sprig of the aromatic leaves. The frothy white flowers are followed by juicy black fruits, which make a delicious jam. The common broad-leaved variety can be damaged by hard frosts, but narrow-leaved *M. c.* subsp. *tarentina* is hardier, if slower growing, with white berries.
Height and spread 3m (10ft)
Hardiness Frost hardy Z9–11

Phillyrea latifolia

This stalwart of the Italian garden, also very popular in 17th-century English gardens, is a slow-growing evergreen shrub that responds well to pruning, making a beautiful, glossy hedge or specimen tree. Plants can cope with sun or shade, but sharp drainage is essential. Generally disease resistant, but look out for white fly on the new leaf tips.
Height and spread To 9m (30ft)
Hardiness Frost hardy Z9–11

Pittosporum tobira
JAPANESE MOCK ORANGE

This outstanding plant is widely used for hedging on the Riviera, due to its resistance to wind and salt. It responds beautifully to cloud-pruning, owing to its graceful, wide-branched habit. The leaves are a shiny, bright green, the flowers white and small, but powerfully honey-scented. Grows well in shade.
Height 1.8–10m (6–33ft); **spread** 1.5–3m (5–10ft)
Hardiness Frost hardy Z9–11

Prunus lusitanica
PORTUGAL LAUREL

This indestructible, vigorous shrub has long, glossy, dark green leaves and highly scented racemes of creamy white flowers in summer. The red fruits that follow ripen to a deep purple. An ideal plant for shallow, chalk soils and always to be preferred to the cherry laurel (*Prunus laurocerasus*).
Height and spread To 20m (70ft)
Hardiness Frost hardy Z7–11

Versatile *Pittosporum tobira* makes a fragrant hedge or shapely tree.

Patio plants that thrive in large pots or containers

Container growing is an opportunity to create combinations of plants that would be impossible in the border, and to nurture treasures that would not thrive on your soil. It also makes it easier to enjoy the beauty of your plants in close-up detail.

Agapanthus
AFRICAN BLUE LILY

Agapanthus comprises ten species of clump-forming perennials, all of which grow well in pots, producing spectacular blue or white flowers in late summer. Keep dry in winter. (See also page 117.)
Height 10cm–2m (4in–6ft)
Hardiness Pot grown agapanthus should be treated as half hardy Z10–11

Asplenium scolopendrium
HART'S TONGUE FERN

Asplenium grows in all continents apart from Antarctica. The wild European fern has evergreen, strap-like, leathery fronds. There are various cultivars, such as narrow-leaved 'Angustatum' and the wavy-edged Crispum Group, but it is hard to beat the tough-as-old-boots species. Cut off the old, browned growth in early spring to encourage young leaves. The more damp and shady you keep it, the lusher it will grow.
Height and spread 34–70cm (13–28in)
Hardiness Hardy Z7–11

Camellia japonica

Worth growing for the beautiful, shiny leaves alone, camellias delight all over again with their glorious flowers. Choose whichever of the smaller cultivars captures your heart and grow in partial shade in ericaceous potting mix. Water well in summer, and prune only to restrict its size.
Height Varies with cultivar, 1.5–3m (5–10ft) for pot-grown specimens
Hardiness Hardy Z7–11

Citrus limon
LEMON

Lemons make delightful pot plants with their glossy fragrant leaves and highly scented flowers, even before they bear fruit, which will often appear alongside the flowers. (See also page 20.)
Height 60cm–2m (2–8ft)
Hardiness Tender to frost hardy Z11

Convolvulus cneorum

This excellent little plant is compact, bushy and tidy in habit, offering shiny, silver foliage all year round and delicate, blush-white, bindweed flowers from spring to mid-summer. A light trim in spring is said to promote more flowers, but save more radical pruning till after flowering. Give it a hot spot in the sun, and good drainage.
Height and spread 75cm (30in)
Hardiness Frost hardy Z9–11

Hosta 'Frances Williams'

This is a chunky plant with thick, quilted, heart-shaped leaves. The centres are a metallic grey-green, with wavy, yellow-lime margins that really glow in a shady position. Greyish-white flowers are held on long stalks in summer. Mulch with horticultural grit or sheep wool, and fix copper tape round the pot to deter slugs. Standing the pot on a copper-impregnated mat may also help – copper gives slugs a mild electric shock.
Height 60cm (2ft); **spread** 1m (39in)
Hardiness Hardy Z8–11

Hydrangea arborescens 'Annabelle'

The smaller hydrangeas grow well in large tubs in ericaceous compost, but do need regular watering and feeding. 'Annabelle' is a well-shaped bushy shrub with attractive serrated leaves and spectacular, lime-white flowerheads up to 30cm (12in) across. Leave them on through the winter, then in early spring cut them back to the first pair of strong buds. At the same time remove any dead, weak or crowded stems, plus one or two of the oldest stems, to encourage strong new shoots that will quickly flower.
Height and spread Up to 3m (10ft)
Hardiness Hardy Z8–11

Lilium
LILY

While the ancient Madonna lily (*L. candidum*), tiger lilies and martagon lilies are happier in the border, the showier, large-flowered oriental and Asiatic lilies all do well in large, deep pots in full sun, if well fed and watered. The oriental lilies are hybrids between Korean *L. speciosum* and the Japanese *L. auratum* – voluptuous creatures growing up to 2m (6½ft) high with blooms in extravagantly striped whites and pinks, and rich, heady perfumes of syrup and clove. The Asiatics are smaller, with virtually no scent, but masses of star-shaped flowers in red, orange, yellow, apricot, peach, and even purple. The stately, white regal lily (*L. regale*) also does well in pots.
Height and spread 45cm–2m (18in–6½ft)
Hardiness Hardy to half hardy Z8–11

Melianthus major
HONEY BUSH

Simply the most beautiful architectural shrub, with large, pinnate fronds of blue-grey leaves with a distinctive scent of chocolate. The dark reddish flowers are borne on upright arching spikes, 1m (3ft) long, in spring. It grows naturally in moist conditions, and will grow more beautifully if you keep it well watered, but tolerates dryness with fortitude. Cut back in early spring or after flowering.
Height and spread To 3m (10ft)
Hardiness Half hardy Z9–11

Nerium oleander
OLEANDER

This drought-tolerant, evergreen shrub, used for roadside plantings throughout the Mediterranean, can be trained into an elegant, multi-stemmed tree that makes a delightful feature on a sheltered patio. It has long, narrow, ribbed leaves and white, red, pink or yellow flowers, blooming from early spring into autumn. Keep it on the dry side, and protect the pot from frost, although the tree is hardy in the ground to -7°C (19°F). All of its parts are very toxic.
Height and spread 1.5m (5ft)
Hardiness Frost tender Z10–11

Pelargonium
GERANIUM

Pelargoniums are the world's favourite pot plants, enjoyed everywhere for their seemingly endless succession of cheerful flowers. (See also page 49.)
Height and spread To 1.5m (5ft)
Hardiness Frost tender Z10

Agapanthus 'Loch Hope'

Hosta 'Frances Williams'

Melianthus major

Nerium oleander

Ceanothus 'Puget Blue'

Fremontodendron californicum 'California Glory'

Wall shrubs and climbers for temperate and Mediterranean gardens

Make the most of vertical space by planting shrubs and climbers that will thrive in the shelter of walls. Fruit trees are not included here, but don't overlook all that trained apples and pears, peaches or apricots can bring to the garden.

Shrubs and climbers for sunny walls

Actinidia deliciosa (syn. *Actinidia chinensis*)
KIWI FRUIT

A vigorous, deciduous, twining climber, with large, rough, heart-shaped leaves on hairy red stems. Fragrant, white flowers are followed, in a warm site, by the familiar, furry, green-fleshed fruit. Male and female plants are needed to produce fruit.
Height 9m (30ft)
Hardiness Frost hardy Z9–11

Bougainvillea

These colourful climbers are a classic choice for warm Mediterranean gardens. (See also page 49.)
Height and spread To 12m (40ft)
Hardiness Frost tender Z10–11

Ceanothus
CALIFORNIAN LILAC

Ceanothus is short-lived (lasting for approximately 10 years), but fast-growing and robust, making excellent spring colour on a sunny, sheltered wall. Blue flowers are borne on stiff, arching branches. Deciduous *C. arboreus* 'Trewithen Blue' is large and spreading, with bright green leaves and vivid, scented flowers; evergreen *C.* 'Puget Blue' is neater and denser growing, with dark, sticky leaves and long-lasting, lapis lazuli flowers; while *C.* 'Zanzibar' bears bright blue flowers on vividly gold-variegated foliage. Always prune straight after flowering – and never into old wood. Evergreens will live longer if left unpruned.
Height and spread 1.5–4m (4½–13ft)
Hardiness Frost hardy Z9–11

Clematis armandii

This vigorous, evergreen climber loves to romp along trellis or over arches, and makes an excellent backdrop for any planting, from jungle giants to herbaceous borders. Masses of highly scented, white or pale pink flowers appear in early spring. It is easy to grow in any type of soil. Pruning is not necessary, unless it goes bare at the base, in which case chop some stems back to fill in with new greenery.
Height 5m (15ft) or more
Hardiness Frost hardy Z8–11

Cytisus battandieri
PINEAPPLE BROOM

A beautiful broom from the Atlas Mountains in Morocco. Racemes of yellow, pineapple-scented flowers appear from early to mid-summer, set off by soft silvery leaves divided into three leaflets. You can train it against a wall and prune back after flowering to keep it neat and small. It is a wonderful sight when planted next to ceanothus.
Height and spread To 3.5m (11½ft)
Hardiness Frost hardy Z8–11

Fremontodendron californicum 'California Glory'
FLANNEL BUSH

This slightly floppy, semi-evergreen shrub is best grown in poor soil, trained against a sunny wall, pruning and tying in the branches to keep it in shape. The dark three-lobed leaves are covered in small hairs, which can cause skin irritation. But its bad habits are soon forgotten when it produces its prolific crop of sunshine-yellow flowers in spring, and it will carry on flowering through the summer.
Height 4m (13ft); **spread** 3m (10ft)
Hardiness Frost hardy Z8–11

Ipomoea
MORNING GLORY

Many of the morning glories prized by gardeners are actually perennials, but are grown as annuals in climes cooler than their tropical homelands. They need a warm, sheltered location in moderately fertile soil, where they will produce their gloriously exotic, bell-like flowers all summer. *I. purpurea* is the common morning glory, with blue, purple and red flowers. More flamboyant cultivars include the deep purple 'Star of Yalta', pink and cerise *I. tricolor* 'Black Knight', dark red 'Crimson Rambler' and the ever-popular 'Heavenly Blue'.
Height 1–3m (3–10ft)
Hardiness Frost tender Z10–11

Jasminum
JASMINE

The common jasmine, *J. officinale*, needs no introduction, with its exquisitely scented, white flowers opening from pink buds. *J. beesianum* has small, deep red flowers, and *J. x stephanense* has pink flowers. Both are vigorous and fragrant. The winter-flowering wall shrub *J. nudiflorum* is not recommended for a small garden, as it is too untidy when not in flower.
Height 2–3m (6½–10ft)
Hardiness Hardy to frost tender Z9–11

Passiflora
PASSIONFLOWER

The hardy *P. caerulea* can grow to cover several houses, sprawling wantonly and seeding about. The species has purple, white and blue flowers; its cultivar 'Constance Elliott' is white; *P.* 'Amethyst' has vivid purple, reflexed petals. *P. x exoniensis* is less hardy, but its rose-pink flowers are abundant. For optimum flowering,

Passiflora caerulea is ideal for a poor, dry spot in the sun.

prune only after growth has restarted in spring, and never cut hard to the main stems. Tidy gardeners should stick with exotic tropical passionflowers, grown in pots and overwintered indoors.
Height and spread Indefinite
Hardiness Hardy to frost tender Z9–11

Trachelospermum jasminoides
STAR JASMINE
A slow, neat, drought-tolerant, evergreen climber with dark, pointed, glossy leaves setting off starry, white flowers in the summer. Resembling jasmine, but much larger, it is strongly fragrant. If you only have room for one climber, this is a superb all-rounder.
Height and spread To 3m (10ft)
Hardiness Frost hardy Z9–11

Vitis vinifera
GRAPE VINE
Most of the hundreds of cultivars will grow successfully in cooler climates, but warmth is needed in summer to sweeten the fruit. Only prune when the plant is dormant, as vines bleed prodigiously. (See also page 20.)
Height and spread Variable
Hardiness Hardy to frost tender Z9–11

Wisteria
With distinctive, long, fragrant racemes of white, pink, blue or lilac pea-flowers, these are the showiest of climbers – rampant, long-lived, and thriving in any soil. Find a sunny site with shade at the roots, water regularly in summer, and prune ruthlessly to limit leafy growth and promote buds. Curiously, *W. floribunda* from Japan twines clockwise, while *W. chinensis* from China twines anti-clockwise.
Height and spread 10–15m (33–50ft)
Hardiness Hardy Z7–11

Shrubs and climbers for shady walls

Akebia quinata
CHOCOLATE VINE
This invaluable, semi-evergreen twiner will grow in any soil, in sun or shade, but is best grown over an arch or trellis where you can enjoy its chocolate scent. Racemes of delicate, burgundy flowers are set off by clusters of bright green leaflets in spring.
Height and spread 5–10m (15–30ft)
Hardiness Hardy Z7–11

Ampelopsis brevipedunculata
PORCELAIN BERRY
The palmate, dark green leaves alone would be reason enough to grow this dense, leafy vine, but its chief beauty is the late-summer berries of astonishing colours, ranging from purple and lilac to cream to swimming-pool turquoise. Tolerant of most soils and some shade.
Height and spread 5m (15ft)
Hardiness Hardy Z7–11

Clematis alpina
ALPINE CLEMATIS
A delicate, well-behaved clematis with fresh green leaves and gently nodding flowers in shades of red, pink, white and blue, which does well in light shade. Like all clematis, it needs to be deeply planted, and needs well-drained, fertile soil to thrive. *C. a.* 'Ruby' is a delightful variety, with soft red flowers with long, cream stamens in late spring. When the flowers fade, exquisite, fluffy seedheads add a second season of interest.
Height and spread 2.5m (8ft)
Hardiness Hardy Z8–11

Hedera
IVY
This undervalued plant is glossy and attractive all year round, unfussy and wildlife-friendly. Even the common *H. helix* is handsome, and there are hundreds of cultivars to offer every effect from clipped curtains of green to sparkling waterfalls of white-splashed foliage; from bushy tumbles of berry-bearing cover to tiny leaves exquisitely crimped and crinkled. 'Sagittifolia' and 'Ivalace' are superlative for form, 'Goldheart' and 'Kolibri' for pattern, 'Glacier' and 'Goldheart' for colour.
Height and spread Varies with variety from 1m (3ft) to indefinite
Hardiness Hardy to half hardy Z8–11

Hydrangea anomala subsp. petiolaris
CLIMBING HYDRANGEA
A large, woody, self-clinging climber, ideal for covering a blank, shady wall. Large, white, airy lace-cap blooms appear in early summer. These dry on the plant to remain through the winter once the leaves have dropped, and, together with the handsome architecture of branches, make it one of the more successful deciduous climbers for winter. Grows vigorously in moist, humus-rich soil –

so be ruthless in cutting back to keep it close to the wall.
Height To 15m (50ft)
Hardiness Hardy Z8–11

Lonicera
HONEYSUCKLE
Most honeysuckles grow well in partial or even full shade, and all prefer shade at the roots. For best results, give them a rich soil that does not dry out in summer, and be alert for aphid attack. As a rule of thumb, you will have to choose between magnificence of bloom or fragrance, but early-flowering creamy-apricot *L. caprifolium* (3m/10ft), clove-scented yellow and pink *L.* x *americana* (6m/20ft) and long-flowering *L. periclymenum* 'Serotina' (4–6m/13–20ft) all offer ravishing scent with a fair amount of flower power, and are trouble-free.
Height and spread As above
Hardiness Hardy to half hardy Z8–11

Rosa
ROSE
In the huge family of roses, you will find many that grow happily in partial shade. Here are just a few for starters. For yellows, try 'Golden Showers', 'The Pilgrim' or 'Teasing Georgia'. For pink: 'Madame Grégoire Staechelin', 'Saint Swithun', 'New Dawn'. 'Paul Noel' is salmon, 'A Shropshire Lad' is peach, 'Tess of the d'Urbervilles' a rich, ruby red, while the ever-popular 'Mme Alfred Carrière' is white, with a faint fleshy blush. All these roses are fragrant – what is the point of a rose without a scent?
Height and spread Varies with cultivar from 1–8m (3–26ft)
Hardiness Hardy to frost hardy Z8–11

Schizophragma hydrangeoides
This is a less vigorous alternative to *Hydrangea anomala* subsp. *petiolaris* – and even lovelier. It grows to about two-thirds of the size, with long, dark green, pointed leaves, red-brown stems and more delicate, white lacecaps. There is also a pink form, 'Roseum'. 'Moonlight' has particularly good leaves – blue-green with pewter markings and dark green veining.
Height and spread To 10m (30ft)
Hardiness Hardy Z9–11

Akebia quinata

Ampelopsis brevipedunculata

Hedera helix 'Goldheart'

Hydrangea petiolaris

Arbutus unedo

Cercis siliquastrum

Ficus carica

Quercus ilex

Drought-tolerant trees for dry summer conditions

While some of the most characteristic trees of the Mediterranean, such as cedar, cork oak, maritime pine and umbrella pine, grow too large for many domestic gardens, there are many good, undemanding, small trees that will do well in dry summer conditions. In a smaller garden, trees have to be all-rounders – so these are selected for elegant form and variety of interest, as well as resilience. See also pages 152–3 for drought-tolerant antipodean trees such as *Acacia dealbata*, *Cordyline australis*, *Eucalyptus* and *Hoheria*.

Arbutus unedo
STRAWBERRY TREE
A marvellous Mediterranean tree with year-round interest, offering attractive, red, peeling bark; dark, leathery evergreen leaves; and drooping panicles of white flowers borne at the same time as the small, red fruits that give it its name. The Latin word *unedo* means 'I eat one' – and indeed one would be plenty of this bitter fruit! Robust, wind-resistant and chalk tolerant, it grows slowly but steadily in softer climates.
Height and spread 2–3m (6½–10ft)
Hardiness Frost hardy Z9–11

Cercis siliquastrum
JUDAS TREE
Legend has it that this is the tree from which Judas hanged himself. This elegant, spreading, usually multi-stemmed tree is grown both for its beautiful, bright green, heart-shaped leaves, which turn butter-yellow in autumn, and for the massive clusters of pinky-purple flowers which burst from the bare stems in spring.
Height and spread To 10m (33ft)
Hardiness Hardy Z7–11

Crataegus orientalis (syn. C. laciniata)
While hawthorns are common in temperate climates, this small tree hails from south-eastern Europe and south-western Asia, and brings a southern elegance with deeply cut, downy leaves that are dark green above and grey beneath. Clusters of white flowers in late spring are followed by coral-red fruits in autumn. This tough little tree will withstand extremes of weather.
Height and spread 6m (20ft)
Hardiness Hardy Z7–11

Ficus carica
COMMON FIG
The fig has been cultivated since ancient times – it was grown by the Egyptians in 4000BC – and grows wild on cliffs and rocks in south-western Asia. These inhospitable conditions must be replicated for success in the garden – if you want good fruit, plant on top of a good helping of rubble, and restrict the roots by sinking paving slabs around the root area. Figs need a warm, sunny spot, and respond well to training on a south wall. The most common variety is 'Brown Turkey', but if you can lay your hands on sumptuous 'Black Ischia', it will make better eating.
Height and spread To 6m (20ft)
Hardiness Hardy Z8–11

Genista aetnensis
MOUNT ETNA BROOM
Found growing in the wild on the islands of Sardinia and Sicily (hence its common name), this is a small, graceful tree, with weeping, rush-like branches which look spectacular wreathed in fragrant, yellow flowers in mid-summer. The effect of the plant is light and airy, casting little shade, so it is ideal for integrating into a planting with other sun lovers beneath.
Height and spread 8m (26ft)
Hardiness Frost hardy Z9–11

Koelreuteria paniculata
GOLDEN RAIN TREE
Hotter, drier summers mean that the lovely golden rain tree can now be grown in temperate gardens. It puts up with drought, poor soil and wind, but needs a good baking to produce its mid-summer showers of golden-yellow flowers, followed by bladder-like fruits.
Height Slowly makes 9m (30ft); **spread** 12m (40ft)
Hardiness Hardy Z9–11

Olea europaea
OLIVE
This archetypal, slow-growing tree of the Mediterranean is becoming an increasingly popular choice for warm urban gardens, where it grows well in poor soil and in pots. (See also page 62.)
Height and spread 10m (30ft)
Hardiness Frost hardy Z8–11

Prunus dulcis
ALMOND
Widely grown for its crop, the almond also makes a beautiful ornamental tree, its blossom traditionally prized in the Islamic garden. (See also page 33.)
Height and spread 8m (25ft)
Hardiness Hardy Z7–11

Quercus ilex
HOLM OAK
This is the tree to leave as your legacy – slow-growing, but magnificent, with attractive, corrugated bark and a mass of shining, dark, evergreen leaves, which can be ovate or lance-shaped, entire or toothed at different stages of development. It thrives in all well-drained soils, and is especially valuable near the coast for its resistance to salt-laden winds. Place it carefully – it is a long-term investment, and casts dense shade. One day it will make 20m (62ft) or more – but not in your lifetime.
Height and spread As above
Hardiness Frost hardy Z8–11

Robinia pseudoacacia
FALSE ACACIA
The mophead acacia is an excellent tree for small town gardens, being slow-growing and tolerant of pollution. The cultivar 'Umbraculifera' makes a compact, lollipop shape ideally suited to sunny, formal gardens, with a dense head of bright green, oval leaflets. It is rather brittle, but in a sheltered urban spot, this is not a problem.
Height and spread 4m (13ft)
Hardiness Hardy Z8–11

Tough shrubs and grasses for dry summer conditions

These drought-tolerant plants and grasses require minimal attention and will not need watering once established. They will all do best in full sun in poor to moderately fertile, free-draining, preferably alkaline soil. A new garden full of builder's rubble is just what they will enjoy. Save your dampest spot for the euphorbia, which will grow lusher as a result: the others will not like it.

Cistus
SUN ROSE, ROCK ROSE

This is the star of the Mediterranean *maquis*, carpeting the hillsides with exquisite, papery, five-petalled blooms, ranging from white to soft pink to deep magenta. Flat, saucer-shaped flowers are creased like tissue paper when they first unfold, and last only for a day. But the plants are so floriferous that there are plenty more each day – valuable colour for the early summer garden. Perhaps the most attractive variety is *C. ladanifer*, the gum cistus, growing to 2m (6½ft), and bearing enormous, white flowers with yellow stamens in the centre, surrounded by five deep, crimson-red blotches. Ladanum, a commercially produced gum, is extracted from the sticky foliage. Follow with slightly smaller and later-flowering *C. x purpureus* with large, splotched, mid-pink flowers.
Height and spread 1.2m (4ft)
Hardiness Frost hardy Z9–11

Euphorbia mellifera
HONEY SPURGE

Here is a shrub to inspire the most reluctant gardener – a magnificent mound of bright green, evergreen foliage, each leaflet with a distinctive creamy midrib. It is hugely architectural, entirely trouble-free and will fill your garden with the scent of honey from handsome, terracotta flowerheads through late spring and early summer. The traditional advice is to grow euphorbia in the shelter of a warm wall, but it is tougher than most people think, taking sharp frosts if they are not prolonged, and needs room to spread and a bit more moisture to give of its best. It can be cut back hard and will quickly rejuvenate from the base.
Height and spread 2–3m (6½ft–10ft)
Hardiness Frost hardy Z9–11

Juniperus
JUNIPER

Evergreens give backbone to a garden, and none more so than the versatile junipers, which come in an array of shapes and sizes for every situation, as well as colours from deepest green to brilliant gold. There are junipers that shoot upward, like *J. scopulorum* 'Sky Rocket', or slower but more pencil-like *J. communis* 'Hibernica' (a good substitute for cypress in a cold climate). There are junipers that grow low but wide, ideal for covering terraces and banks – try dove-grey *J. horizontalis* 'Bar Harbour' or steely blue *J. squamata* 'Blue Carpet'. There are also those that squat toad-like in rockeries, reaching perhaps 70cm (28in) in 20 years. At least, like all junipers, they smell good.
Height and spread Varies with variety: height 10m (30ft); spread 4m (12ft) (*J. scopulorum*); height 3–5m (10–15ft); spread 13cm (12in) (*J. horizontalis*)
Hardiness Hardy to frost hardy Z7–11

Origanum laevigatum 'Herrenhausen'
ORNAMENTAL MARJORAM

Small, round, purple-flushed leaves are topped, in late summer, by dense clusters of tiny, deep pink flowers with deep purple calices, borne on red-purple stems. As it matures, the foliage turns dark green. It makes an ideal edging for a patio, herb garden or well-drained border. Cut back the old, faded flowerheads and stems in spring. Other good varieties are the lighter and pinker 'Hopleys' and taller, burgundy-flowered 'Rosenkuppel'. All are very attractive to butterflies.
Height 60cm (24in), forms spreading mats
Hardiness Hardy Z8–11

Cistus ladanifer bears paper-thin flowers 10cm (4in) across.

Phlomis fructicosa
JERUSALEM SAGE

Grown in gardens for over 400 years, Jerusalem sage grows wild on rocky hillsides, and does well on dry banks and in well-drained, limey soils. It makes an ever-grey bush about 1.5m (5ft) round, and bears long-lasting whorls of rich yellow flowers. It can, however, become leggy and bare at the base unless regularly pruned, and is prone to a rust-like spotting. Its smaller (30cm/12in) relative *P. italica* is altogether better behaved, with hairy, silvery stems and terminal spikes of pale lilac flowers in summer.
Height and spread As above
Hardiness Hardy to frost hardy Z8–11

Euphorbia mellifera

Punica granatum
POMEGRANATE

Highly prized in the Islamic garden (see also page 33), the pomegranate is known as the 'Jewel of Winter', its bright red flowers followed by shiny red fruits from September to November in the northern hemisphere and March to May in the southern hemisphere.
Height and spread 2–8m (6–25ft)
Hardiness Hardy Z8–11

Phlomis fructicosa

Rhamnus alaternus
'Argenteovariegata'

Rosa glauca

Rhamnus alaternus 'Argenteovariegata'
ITALIAN BUCKTHORN

An invaluable foliage shrub, with a soft cream and green variegation, that also does well in semi-shade. Protect from strong winds.
Height and spread 2m (6½ft)
Hardiness Frost hardy Z9–11

Rosa
ROSE

Although we tend to think of roses as delicate, demanding creatures, typical of the English garden, roses are widely grown in Mediterranean and Islamic gardens (see page 33), and there are many shrub roses in particular that are tough as old boots. In southern France and Italy, *R. mutabilis* flowers for nine months of the year, changing colour from light yellow to pale copper to deep pink, while spring is ushered in by cascades of *Rosa banksia*. *R. glauca* has beautiful, grey foliage and showy, red hips in addition to papery summer flowers. The many forms of *R. rugosa* are so accommodating that they are frequently used in supermarket plantings, while the wild, white, burnet rose, *R. pimpinellifolia*, makes a beautiful, small-growing shrub for a difficult bank.
Height and spread Varies with variety
Hardiness Hardy to frost hardy Z8–11

Rosmarinus officinalis
ROSEMARY

Backbone of the herb garden, fragrant evergreen rosemary also performs well in mixed plantings and prostrate forms make ideal groundcover for difficult dry banks. (See also page 62.)
Height and spread To 2m (6ft)
Hardiness Frost hardy Z7–11

Spartium junceum
SPANISH BROOM

A strongly growing shrub with green, rush-like stems; small, inconspicuous leaves; and a loose habit that can become lax in too well-fed and sheltered a spot. Prune hard but carefully in early spring – never going into the old wood – to keep it upright. The fragrant, yellow, pea flowers appear in large terminal clusters in summer, and last well into the autumn.
Height To 3m (10ft); **spread** 2–5m (6½–16½ft)
Hardiness Frost hardy Z9–11

Tamarix
TAMARISK

This is a real survivor, capable of withstanding the roughest winds, the most alkaline or saline soils, drought and inundation. It is frequently planted as a windbreak in coastal situations. Feathery, pink flowers and plume-like foliage dance in the wind on slender, whippy branches, lasting for months at a time. Treat it mean – if given too sheltered a billet it will need hard pruning. *T. ramosissima* 'Rubra' is the best coloured and neatest variety.
Height 4.5m (15ft); **spread** 3m (10ft)
Hardiness Hardy Z8–11

Zauschneria californica 'Dublin'
CALIFORNIAN FUCHSIA

A small, sprawling, blue-grey Chaparral shrub, which bursts into flaming, scarlet colour in late summer, covered in masses of funnel-shaped flowers till the first frosts. A brilliant boost to the late-summer garden. Prune lightly in spring if required for tidiness.
Height and spread 30cm (12in)
Hardiness Hardy (borderline) Z9–11

Grasses

See also the New Zealand grasses mentioned on page 108.

Calamagrostis x acutifolia 'Karl Foerster'
FEATHER REED GRASS

A strongly architectural cool season grass starting early into growth, making dense clumps. (See also page 77.)
Height To 1.5m (5ft)
Hardiness Frost hardy Z6–10

Elymus magellanicus
BLUE WHEAT GRASS

The bluest of all the blue grasses, with wide foliage, forming slowly spreading clumps. (See also page 77.)
Height 40–50cm (16–20in)
Hardiness Frost hardy Z5

Oryzopsis miliacea
INDIAN RICE GRASS

A fast-growing, drought-resistant Mediterranean grass flowering from mid-summer with huge airy panicles. (See also page 77.)
Height To 60cm (2ft); **spread** 30cm (12in)
Hardiness Frost hardy Z5

Panicum virgatum 'Heavy Metal'
PRAIRIE SWITCH GRASS

Tight, stiff clumps of grey-blue leaves, stems and flowers. Foliage turns butter-yellow in autumn. (See also page 77.)
Height To 1m (3ft)
Hardiness Frost hardy Z6

Stipa gigantea
GOLDEN OAT GRASS

Evergreen basal clumps of narrow foliage produce striking tall heads of light golden brown buff flowers lasting for many months. It must have a sunny, well-drained spot. (See also page 77.)
Height To 2m (6½ft)
Hardiness Frost hardy Z7–10

Stipa tenuissima 'Pony Tails'
FEATHER GRASS

Soft, dense clumps of fine hair-like evergreen foliage with lighter green flowers in summer, turning gently to beige. This grass is a graceful companion for almost everything. Best in poor soil in sun. (See also page 77.)
Height to 2m (6½ft)
Hardiness Fully hardy to frost tender Z6

Colourful *Zauschneria californica* lasts well into autumn.

Silver foliage for drought conditions

Adapted by nature to deal with long periods of drought and thin, stony soils, grey and silver-foliage plants will keep your garden in good shape throughout the fiercest summer. All they require is a position in full sun and good drainage, especially in winter – dry cold will not kill them, but waterlogging will.

Artemisia
WORMWOOD, SOUTHERNWOOD
This family, more than any other, gives a range of beautiful, silver foliage to the garden, and is usually strongly scented. *A. abrotanum* is a traditional cottage-garden favourite, with finely divided, grey, downy leaves and dull yellow flowers. *A. absinthium* is the source of absinthe – the best cultivar is 'Lambrook Silver', with finely cut, very silver leaves. *A. ludoviciana* 'Valerie Finnis' is a fine plant, with long, pointed, notched leaves which are almost white. *A. arborescens* 'Faith Raven' is the largest of the group with a height and spread of 1.2m (4ft), while finely fronded *A. schmidtiana* makes a low mat some 10–30cm (4–12in) high, ideal for a scree garden. If you can only have one, go for *A.* 'Powis Castle', with deeply cut, silver-blue, ferny foliage. It does not flower – an advantage in artemisias – and this helps it retain a neater habit.
Height and spread As above
Hardiness Hardy to frost hardy Z9–11

Ballota pseudodictamnus
Low-growing, ever-grey shrub with rounded, fine, white-furred leaves and stems. Small, pink flowers with large, pale green calyces are held in whorls towards the stem tips. For best foliage, cut back in spring before it starts into growth.
Height 50cm (20in) (but can be trained higher); **spread** 60cm (2ft)
Hardiness Hardy (borderline) Z9–11

Helianthemum
ROCK ROSE
Closely related to cistus, the easy-going rock roses sprawl attractively over stony ground, sprinkled with papery blooms from early summer onwards. There are many, many cultivars, ranging from palest pink to blood-curdling orange. The glowing, white blooms of 'The Bride' are especially attractive, as are the 'Wisley' cultivars in delicate shades of pink and primrose. Cut back hard after flowering to keep them neat.
Height 20cm (8in); **spread** 30cm (12in) plus, but varies with variety
Hardiness Hardy to frost hardy Z9–11

Helichrysum italicum
CURRY PLANT
The narrow, silvery-grey leaves of this dense, dwarf sub-shrub smell strongly of curry. Small, everlasting, bright yellow flowers are produced in summer. *H. italicum* subsp. *microphyllum* has especially bright foliage, but is more tender than the species.
Height and spread 60cm (2ft)
Hardiness Frost hardy Z9–11

Lavandula
LAVENDER
Invaluable scented herb, ornamental and hedge. (See also page 62.)
Height and spread 60cm (2ft) (*L. angustifolia*); 45cm (18in) (*L. stoechas*)
Hardiness Hardy to half hardy Z6–9

Romneya coulteri
TREE POPPY
This gorgeous sub-shrub, native to southern California, is grown for its lustrous, light grey, frondy foliage and its enormous, white, poppy-like flowers. It prefers more fertile soil than most grey-leaved plants, and the delicate summer flowers, with their intense yellow centres, last better out of the wind. Difficult to establish, but once content it will spread around freely. 'White Cloud' is a strong-growing form.
Height and spread 2m (6½ft)
Hardiness Frost hardy Z9–11

Salvia argentea
Rosette-forming perennial grown for its woolly, silver foliage, impossible to pass without stroking. Strong, upright stems suddenly appear in summer, carrying dainty, white flowers.
Height 1m (3ft); **spread** 60cm (24in)
Hardiness Hardy Z9–11

Salvia officinalis
COMMON SAGE
Sage has been valued for thousands of years for its healing and culinary properties. Soft, grey-green mounds of foliage set off pretty, blue flowers in summer – variegated, purple, red and multi-coloured versions are also available. Chop back hard after flowering to contain its spread, or it will get woody and sprawly. Sage roots easily from cuttings, so it is worth replacing plants every five years or so, when they get too untidy.
Height 75cm (2½ft); **spread** 1m (3ft)
Hardiness Hardy Z8–11

Santolina chamaecyparissus
COTTON LAVENDER
A valuable, mound-forming plant with finely divided, silvery foliage, studded with yellow, button flowers in summer. These can sometimes be a rather coarse mustard colour, but 'Lemon Queen' is more refined. 'Lambrook Silver' is an especially silver form. There is also a green form, *S. rosmarinifolia* subsp. *rosmarinifolia* (syn. *S. virens*), which makes a good foil for the ever-greys.
Height 50cm (20in); **spread** 1m (3ft)
Hardiness Frost hardy Z9–11

Stachys byzantina
LAMBS' EARS, LAMBS' LUGS
A half-hardy, mat-forming perennial grown principally for its large, soft, woolly leaves. These are very liable to rot in wet conditions, so find it the best-drained spot you can, and give it a dry mulch round the crown to see it through the winter. 'Silver Carpet' is a popular, non-flowering variety, and more shade-tolerant than many other silver plants. However, the soft, lilac flower spikes make an attractive feature at the front of the border.
Height 30cm (1ft); **spread** 60cm (2ft)
Hardiness Hardy Z9–11

Teucrium fruticans
SHRUBBY GERMANDER
Germander makes a beautiful, low-growing hedge in the manner of lavender, or use it in a mixed planting where its soft, felted, silvery leaves can be a foil for more spiky planting. As well as lovely, fragrant foliage, it has pale blue flowers that bloom for several months from early spring. An excellent seaside plant.
Height 1m (3ft); **spread** 4m (13ft)
Hardiness Frost hardy Z9–11

Helichrysum italicum

Helianthemum 'Wisley Pink'

Artemisia

Stachys byzantina

Acanthus mollis

Aeonium arboreum
'Atropurpureum'

Accent plants for dry gardens

When planning a dry garden, you will need accent plants among the softer, mound-forming ones to underpin and give vigour to the scheme. Succulents and spiky plants are excellent for this, as are the suggestions below. All prefer full sun in light, well-drained soil, unless otherwise indicated.

Acanthus
BEAR'S BREECHES
This is the original architectural plant – its leaves are carved on the columns of ancient Greece. Semi-evergreen perennial *A. mollis* has large, shiny, deeply cut oval leaves, while *A. spinosus* has spiny, serrated leaves with prickly tips. Both bear hefty spikes of blue and white flowers in late summer. It will grow in sun or shade, but needs plenty of air circulation to avoid mildew, which can be a problem when it gets very dry. Be sure to plant it exactly where you want it, and give it lots of room. It is rather a thug, and will regenerate from the smallest fragment of root, so is impossible to move.
Height and spread 1.2m (4ft)
Hardiness Hardy to frost tender Z9–11

Aeonium
Evergreen perennials, grown for their succulent rosettes of waxy leaves, which may be green, purple or attractively variegated. Some are shrubby in form, whereas others hug the ground (see also page 95). All should be watered sparingly, drying out between waterings, and kept above 5°C (41°F) so are best grown in pots, and set out in the garden just for the summer months, but many will survive brief frosts given excellent drainage.
Height and spread To 1m (3ft) with rosettes 15–20cm across (*A. arboreum*)
Hardiness Frost tender Z11

Allium
Round heads of alliums floating above mounds of foliage make a real statement in the garden. Leave the seedheads as long as you can – good structure for the planting, and a source of food for wildlife. 'Firmament' and 'Purple Sensation' are robust and long-lasting.
Height Varies with variety
Hardiness Hardy to frost hardy Z8–11

Cynara cardunculus
CARDOON
The most architectural of the grey-leaved plants, with leaves up to 90cm (3ft) long emerging early in the season. In late summer it produces tall flowering stalks, bearing immense, purple, thistle flowers. The young leaves may be blanched and eaten.
Height 2m (6½ft)
Hardiness Hardy Z8–11

Echium pininana
This wonderful exhibitionist from the Canary Isles throws up colossal spikes of electric blue flowers up to 4m (13ft) high, held above basal rosettes of coarse, hairy leaves up to 90cm (3ft) across. There are over 40 species of *Echium*, from annuals and biennials to perennial herbs and sub-shrubs, which will seed around if happy. Echiums can take some shade, but do need protection from wind and frost, so gather up a few seedlings as back-up.
Height As above
Hardiness Frost hardy Z10–11

Eremurus
FOXTAIL LILY
Native to central Asia, *Eremurus* are known there as 'desert candles' – well-spaced columns of fiery, star-shaped blooms soaring from a basal rosette. They are not easy to grow – plant them out on a 10cm (4in) bed of horticultural grit in autumn, with their crowns poking up above the soil, and protect from winter wet. Nor are they long in flower – just three weeks in summer. But place a group of orange *E.* x *isabellinus* 'Cleopatra' near your alliums, or dark yellow *E. stenophyllus* with your euphorbias, and you will think them well worth the effort.
Height 1.2m (4ft); **spread** 60cm (2ft)
Hardiness Hardy Z9–11

Eryngium giganteum
MISS WILLMOTT'S GHOST
Long-lasting and superbly sculptural, sea hollies make outstanding accent plants. Their only drawback is that they die most unattractively. Most striking are the silvery biennial *E. giganteum* and the smaller deciduous perennials in shades of icy blue, such as vivid *E. bourgatii, E. tripartitum* with smaller, daintier heads and the larger-headed *E.* x *oliverianum*. (See also page 81.)
Height 60cm–1.2m (23–47in); **spread** 50–75cm (20in–2½ft)
Hardiness Hardy Z7–11

Euphorbia characias
SPURGE
Valued by the Greeks for their purgative properties, spurges grow all over the Mediterranean. With their columns of dark, evergreen, generally glaucous leaves, they bring drama and structure to the garden. There are dozens of forms of *E. characias* and its subspecies *wulfenii*, some admired for the brightness of their inflorescences (such as 'John Tomlinson' and 'Lambrook Gold') and some for the colour of their foliage, such as blue-green *E. c.* 'Portuguese Velvet'.

Allium hollandicum 'Purple Sensation'

All are superb, giving months and months of interest. Remove the spent flower stems at the base when they dry up, being careful to avoid the plant's irritant sap.
Height and spread To 1.5m (5ft)
Hardiness Frost hardy Z9–11

Gaura lindheimeri

Some plants command by their statuesque form – *Gaura* enchants with its movement – a summer-long swirl of butterfly flowers dancing in the breeze. Try to get the original form with white flowers on wiry red stems, which can (but rarely do) grow to 1.2m (4ft) high. (Squat pink garden centre versions don't have the same appeal.) It must have good drainage to survive the winter, and benefits from being cut back in spring for tidier, more floriferous growth. An essential plant for the dry garden.
Height and spread To 1m (3ft)
Hardiness Hardy Z9–11

Geranium maderense

This spectacular perennial is a native of Madeira where it is common in gardens and on verges, but now very rare in the wild. It grows successfully outdoors in south-west England. Over the first three or four years of its life, it does not flower. Instead, deeply toothed leaves, up to 50cm (20in) long, with red stalks, form a large rosette. As the lower leaves die back, they bend back, but remain stiff, forming a central trunk that is supported, as if on guy ropes. From the top of this, when the plant has reached flowering size, erupts a massive panicle of vivid magenta flowers, which last a good three months over early summer. The seeds, flung far and wide at the end of the summer, are hardier than the plant, and germinate readily.
Height and spread To 1.2m (4ft)
Hardiness Half hardy Z10–11

Perovskia 'Blue Spire'
RUSSIAN SAGE

An indispensable all-rounder, with cool silver foliage, violet-blue flowers in late summer, strong grey stems that give structure through the winter, and an airy, see-through look that brings a lightness to every planting.

Eryngium giganteum or Miss Willmott's ghost has pale silver flower heads and spiny bracts.

It appears to put up with anything: shade, salt, drought and cold – even rabbits.
Height 1.2m (4ft); **spread** 90cm (3ft)
Hardiness Hardy Z 8–11

Verbascum olympicum
OLYMPIC MULLEIN

A most imposing plant, shooting from a large, grey-felted rosette of basal leaves. The flowering stem branches near the base, giving the effect of an enormous candelabra, and bears numerous bright golden-yellow flowers, 2.5cm (1in) or so across, from mid-summer to autumn. (See also page 81.)
Height 2m (6½ft); **spread** 60cm (24in)
Hardiness Hardy Z8–11

Verbena bonariensis

With its graceful habit, long flowering season (from mid-summer well into autumn) and obliging way of seeding about, this superb plant is equally at home in naturalistic and formal border plantings. (See also page 81.)
Height To 2m (6½ft); **spread** 45cm (18in)
Hardiness Borderline hardy Z9–11

Euphorbia characias subsp. *wulfenii*

Fynbos plants for poor, thin soils

While restios are becoming better known in American and European gardens, few of us dare to grow leucadendrons or proteas. But why not? If we can attempt Mediterranean shrubs, then it is also worth experimenting with these exotic and colourful plants from South Africa's Cape, called fynbos. Key to success is sun, good air circulation and a soil low in phosphates and nitrates.

Erica cerinthoides

Leucospermum cordifolium

Leucadendron argenteum

Protea cynaroides

Erica

CAPE HEATH

While Europe can muster only 21 species of heath flora, South Africa proffers over 400, in a vast array of forms and colours. *E. gracilis* is a compact (30cm/12in) plant grown for winter display, while *E. canaliculata* bears a profusion of pale pink, cup-shaped flowers in late winter to spring, and can grow as high as 2m (6½ft). This species can withstand -7°C (19°F) air frosts but is destroyed by -11°C (12°F) air frosts. *E. cerinthoides* has narrow leaves and compact spikes of tubular flowers, produced in shades of red, pink or white from winter to spring, while *E. versicolor* is taller and even more handsome, its long, red, tubular flowers tipped with yellow. All are undemanding and drought-tolerant, preferring poor, well-drained soil, but they are not long-lived and can expire suddenly.

Height and spread As above
Hardiness Hardy to frost tender Z9–11

Leucadendron

This beautiful group of mostly evergreen plants is closely related to the proteas, but bears highly coloured bracts instead of showy flowers. They do best on poor, nutrient-starved soils. Leucadendrons are dioecious, meaning male and female flowers are borne on separate plants. *L. gandogeri* reaches about 2m (6½ft) tall, bearing soft, limey, daisy-shaped bracts. *L. xanthoconas* has starry clusters of soft lemon green, and papery 'buds' like little bonbons. A common fynbos plant, it makes a great foil for showier plantings. *L. tinctum* has yellow male flowerheads, while the female flowerhead is a shiny maroon. Flowers have a pleasant, spicy, musk scent, lending it its common name of 'spicy conebush'.

Perhaps the showiest of them all is *L. argenteum*, the silver tree. This glorious tree, reaching 10m (30ft) in its native habitat, grows only in the Cape Peninsula, where it is increasingly threatened by urban development. The symmetrical, upright branches are coated with tightly overlapping, grey-green leaves, covering the stem. The leaves are covered with fine hairs that reflect the light, giving them a startlingly brilliant, silvery sheen. It flowers in spring, bearing silvery 'cones' – the female ones being bigger than the male ones. Silver trees like full sun, good drainage, adequate water and above all, good air circulation, seeming to need to blow about in the wind. Thus, they do very well by the sea in south-west England, the Isles of Scilly and the western coasts of Europe.

Height and spread As above
Hardiness Frost tender Z9–11

Leucospermum

PINCUSHION PLANT

Another member of the protea family, *Leucospermum* have rounded flowerheads, tightly packed with bright red, orange or yellow flowers, distinguished by long 'pins' protruding from each flower. *L. cordifolium* is grown as a cut flower for its vivid architectural blooms, but also makes a highly decorative, rounded shrub.

Height and spread To 1.2m (4ft) (*L. cordifolium*)
Hardiness Frost tender Z9–11

Protea

There are around 115 species of *Protea*, growing mostly in the winter rainfall area of Cape Province. Their name comes from the shape-changing Greek god Proteus, and suggests the bewildering variety of forms: while some grow into small trees, most are low, evergreen shrubs, and some, known as snow proteas, sprawl along the ground. Their striking blooms are flowerheads containing a cluster of individual flowers – larger flowerheads may be made up of 200 to 300 florets.

By far the best known is *P. cynaroides*, the king protea, with the largest head of all the proteas, growing to 30cm (12in) across. It is a highly prized cut flower. In the wild, it grows to 3m (10ft) high, but is regularly cut down by fire and resprouts quickly from a woody, underground tuber. Lovelier still is dark red *P. longifolia*, with narrow leaves; long, slightly curled outer petals just like feathers; and a soft, downy centre. *P. eximia* has pink flowerheads and waxy, oblong, sedum-type leaves. Growing above the snow-line, it is perhaps the hardiest of the proteas for the temperate garden. *P. roupelliae* is yellow at the base with red, spoon-shaped petals, with a white margin to pink, sheathed petals.

Proteas need well-drained, sandy, acid soil, spring moisture, and an uncrowded position with plenty of sun and good air circulation – an open, sunny slope is ideal. While some measure of frost protection will be needed, they will survive lows of -6.5°C (20°F) overnight. Avoid artificial fertilizers, but the odd dressing of wood ash is beneficial.

Height and spread As above
Hardiness Half hardy to frost tender Z9–11

Restio

CAPE REEDS

South African restios, with their fine architecture, are gaining in popularity. Some, like *Chondropetalum tectorum*, have tufts of growth resembling juncus, while others, like *Elegia capensis* and *E. fenestrata*, look more like giant horsetails. Giants of the group *Rhodocoma gigantea* and *Calopsis paniculata* offer arching, feathery foliage and bamboo-like stems reaching up to 3m (10ft).

Though newcomers to temperate gardens, restios are proving satisfyingly hardy, surviving lows of -11°C (12°F) with a thick winter mulch or covering of fleece. They are cool-season growers, putting on most growth in early spring and autumn, and 'resting' in the summer. This growth can be fast, with some capable of putting on 1.8–2.7m (6–9ft) stems in one year. Feathery juvenile growth is gradually replaced with mature stems, producing attractive seedheads and beautiful, golden brown, papery bracts.

Like the other fynbos plants, they require an open, sunny position, not crowded by other plants, in free-draining, nutrient-poor soil.

Height and spread As above
Hardiness Fully hardy Z8

South African bulbs for full sun

Here are bulbs and corms to bring real glamour to the garden, adding welcome colour late in the season. Despite their delicate appearance, most are easy to grow. They thrive in full sun and multiply quickly. Buy good-sized bulbs from a specialist supplier.

Amaryllis belladonna
BELLADONNA LILY

This is a popular indoor plant, grown for its large, pink, funnel-shaped flowers which appear before the leaves. It also looks well in the garden, planted among low-growing shrubs in the shelter of a warm wall. Plant out the bulbs in late summer with the necks at soil level, and they will flower in autumn till the first frosts. The bulb is frost hardy, but the fleshy foliage will need protection if a prolonged cold snap is expected.
Height 60cm (24in)
Hardiness Frost hardy Z10–11

Babiana
BABOON FLOWER

It seems unfair that this most graceful of winter-growing plants should have such an ugly name – it derives from the monkey's habit of digging up the corms to eat them. It grows well in rocky situations in mild coastal areas, but needs moisture in the growing season, and protection from frosts, so it may be best grown in pots in a greenhouse in colder, wetter climates. There are around 65 species and many cultivars, usually yellow or mauve, but B. stricta is the most widely available.
Height 15–30cm (6–12in)
Hardiness Frost tender Z9–11

Crocosmia
MONTBRETIA

With strappy leaves in green or bronze, and flowers in a range of fiery shades, montbretias make an invaluable addition to the late summer garden. (See also page 120.)
Height 30cm–1.2m (12in–4ft)
Hardiness Frost hardy Z6–9

Dierama
ANGEL'S FISHING ROD

D. pulcherrimum has become a very fashionable plant, but is not easy to grow. Flower stems rise above a rosette of dark green, linear, evergreen leaves, arching beneath a cargo of delicate bell flowers, varying in colour from magenta to a delicate shell-pink. The plants make corms, but sulk mightily when divided or moved. The ideal plant to grow by butyl-lined ponds, for although it looks beautiful by water and needs summer moisture, it actually requires a well-drained position.
Height 1.5m (5ft)
Hardiness Frost hardy Z9–11

Eucomis
PINEAPPLE FLOWER, PINEAPPLE LILY

Varying greatly in colour and size, the flower spikes of Eucomis are topped with distinctive bracts that give them a resemblance to pineapples. A plant for the eye rather than the nose! (See also page 120.)
Height 8cm–1.8m (3in–6ft)
Hardiness Hardy to frost hardy Z8–11

Galtonica candicans

Late-summer-flowering G. candicans is the most elegant of bulbs, with tall towers of white, waxy bells on sturdy stems held above shiny, blue-green leaves. It is perfectly hardy if planted deeply in soil that does not get waterlogged in winter, although it likes some summer moisture, and will seed around when happy. Use it as an accent plant to take over from alliums. Lime green G. viridiflora is also very fine.
Height 1m (3ft)
Hardiness Hardy Z9–11

Gladiolus

Lose all thoughts of the coarse, blowsy giants beloved of allotmenteers. With more than 250 species, the genus Gladiolus is the largest in the iris family, and the many small species from South Africa make some of the most exquisite flowers in the garden. G. callianthus, still sometimes sold as Acidanthera murielae, has long-tubed, scented, white flowers, with a wine-dark star at the throat. G. papilio spreads by underground runners, and produces dusty purple flowers with golden centres. Both should be planted in spring to flower in summer. G. tristis bears a profusion of greenish-yellow flowers on rush-like stems, and is winter-growing, planted in late summer to flower in spring. It is best grown in the greenhouse, but other gladioli will thrive in a sheltered spot in moisture-retentive soil. Easy-to-please Gladiolus communis subsp. byzantinus flowers in early summer.
Height 80cm–1.7m
Hardiness Hardy to frost tender Z9–11

Kniphofia
RED HOT POKER, TORCH LILY

Spectacular members of the lily family, clump-forming perennials bearing dramatic spikes of often bi-coloured flowers. (See also page 121.)
Height 60cm–1.5m (2–5ft)
Hardiness Hardy to frost hardy Z8–11

Nerine

A genus of about 30 species of bulbs found on well-drained sites on cliffs, rocky ledges and mountain screes in southern Africa. (See also page 121.)
Height 45cm (18in)
Hardiness Frost hardy to frost tender Z9–11

Schizostylis
KAFFIR LILY

Invaluable for late season colour, with dainty flower spikes lasting through to the first frosts. (See also page 121.)
Height 60cm (2ft); **spread** 23cm (9in) (S. coccinea)
Hardiness Frost hardy Z9–11

Strelitzia reginae
BIRD OF PARADISE FLOWER

An evergreen, clump-forming perennial prized for its colourful, beak-shaped inflorescences made up of brilliant orange sepals and vivid purple petals in boat-shaped bracts. Place outside in summer, but overwinter indoors.
Height 1.2 (4ft)
Hardiness Frost tender Z10–11

Watsonia
BUGLE LILY

Evergreen sword-shaped leaves with flower stems of predominantly orange and pink rising above the foliage. (See also page 121.)
Height 1–1.5m (3–5ft)
Hardiness Hardy to Z7 (W. pillansii). Others are tender but should survive with winter protection.

Babiana stricta

Dierama pulcherrimum

Gladiolus byzantinus

Nerine bowdenii 'Silver Smith'

Southern hemisphere plants for the northern hemisphere

Many wonderful plants native to Australia and New Zealand are already proving their worth at home, and, increasingly, in northern hemisphere gardens – but there are more to try. These are selected primarily for foliage interest, but some have excellent flowers too.

Astelia chathamica

Cordyline australis

Eucalyptus glaucescens

Callistemon subulatus

Acacia
WATTLE
Australian acacias make large evergreen shrubs or small trees, with feathery, filigree foliage, and masses of yellow flowers. Best grown on acid or neutral soil (not suitable for chalk). *A. dealbata*, the florist's mimosa, has silvery-green, fern-like leaves and highly scented, fluffy, gold flowers in early spring. Cootamundra wattle (*A. baileyana*) has bluer foliage: the cultivar 'Purpurea' is especially attractive. Oven's wattle (*A. pravissima*) has curious little triangular leaves and an attractive, weeping habit. Drought-tolerant.
Height and spread Various
Hardiness Half hardy to frost tender (mimosa is hardier, surviving -12°C/10°F for short periods) Z9–11

Astelia
A. chathamica, often sold as *A.* 'Silver Spear', is a clump-forming perennial with sword-shaped leaves of sparkling silver up to 2m (6½ft) long. It will grow best in semi-shade and prefers a rich soil but can tolerate some dryness. Its cousin *A. nervosa* is smaller and less silvery, but much hardier and excellent in deep, dry shade. Both regrow quite happily if cut down by frost.
Height and spread 2m (6½ft)
Hardiness Frost hardy to half hardy Z8–11

Callistemon
BOTTLEBRUSH
Native to Australia, *C. subulatus* is one of the hardiest of the 30 species – an evergreen shrub with distinctive, arching branches and crimson 'bottlebrush' flowers. It can cope with most soils, including heavy clay, but dislikes cold winds.
Height and spread 1.5m (5ft) (*C. subulatus*); 5m (15ft) (*C. viminalis*)
Hardiness Hardy to frost tender Z9–11

Celmisia
NEW ZEALAND DAISY
This hardy daisy has striking, silver-green leaves that are slightly furry to the touch. The plant is found all over the country, but particularly in mountainous areas among rocks and stony outcrops. An alpine plant, it needs free-draining, gritty soil. Drought-tolerant.
Height To 15cm (6in); **spread** To 20cm (8ft)
Hardiness Hardy Z7–11

Coprosma
The 45 species from New Zealand range from trees to low-growing shrubs. Many have a divaricating habit. The many varieties offer features such as very shiny or brightly coloured foliage. *C. acerosa* is an outstanding ground-cover plant with springy mounds of interlacing branches. *C.* 'Karo Red' is a compact shrub with small, wine-red leaves; *C.* 'Cutie' is a combination of chocolate and green, *C.* 'Evening Glow' is golden in summer, turning orange and red in winter. For berries, you need both male and female plants.
Height and spread To 2m (6ft)
Hardiness Frost hardy to half hardy Z9–11

Cordyline australis
NEW ZEALAND CABBAGE PALM
A favourite container plant for patio and deck, cordylines are equally good in the border, their eye-catching rosettes of arching leaves giving a boost to modern plantings. One of the largest of the lily family, it bears highly scented flowers in summer. The central bud and the bases of the young leaves, eaten raw or roasted in embers, were a Maori delicacy. Numerous brightly coloured cultivars are available; the darker ones seem to be a bit less hardy, and will need frost protection if grown in pots.
Height To 9m (30ft); **spread** 3m (10ft)
Hardiness Half hardy Z9–11

Dianella nigra (syn. D. intermedia)
This tufted plant offers all-year-round form. The insignificant flowers are followed by superb, dark blue berries in autumn. Likes sun or semi-shade.
Height and spread 60cm (2ft)
Hardiness Half hardy Z9–11

Eucalyptus
GUM TREE, IRONBARK
Potentially very large, the foliage of most species changes shape as the tree matures. Either prune regularly to shrub size and enjoy the silvery, rounded juvenile foliage, or give it room to grow into a noble forest tree. (See also page 108.)
Height 30m (100ft); **spread** 20m (70ft)
Hardiness Mostly frost hardy Z9–11

Grevillea rosmarinifolia
Ideal for hot, sunny sites on poor, sandy soil, this narrow-leaved shrub resembles a large rosemary, but has a stupendous display of honeysuckle-like, crimson flowers in mid-summer. Avoid too much fertilizer. Drought-tolerant.
Height 5m (16ft); **spread** 3m (10ft)
Hardiness Frost hardy Z8–11

Griselinia littoralis
Ideal for seaside plantings, this makes an excellent hedge or backdrop plant with its dense growth of thick, gloss, green leaves and sculptural branching habit. It is fast growing, unfussy as to soil and tolerates light shade. Avoid the variegated forms – the apple-green species is best. Drought-tolerant.
Height and spread 3m (10ft)
Hardiness Hardy (borderline) Z8–11

Hebe
The genus includes plants of shrubby and sprawling growth as well as small trees, but gardeners generally go for small bushes of rounded habit and dense, attractive foliage. Late summer flowers are a bonus. Among the staggering array of cultivars, largish *H. parviflora* var. *angustifolia* (2m/6½ft) has the most desirable habit of thriving in dry shade. *H. cupressoides* 'Boughton Dome' is a useful, small, round ball of tidy green (with a height and spread of 50cm/20in) while *H. epacridea* is a conversation-piece alpine, growing only a few centimetres high, with oblong, rigid leaves.
Height and spread As above
Hardiness Hardy to half hardy Z8–11

Hoheria populnea
LACEBARK
A graceful, evergreen tree. Initial growth is quick, but slows as it matures. It has pretty, serrated leaves and starry, white flowers in summer. Ideal for screening or boundary planting. A good seaside plant.
Height 6m (20ft); **spread** 3m (10ft)
Hardiness Frost hardy Z8–11

Leptospermum
TEA TREE
The manuka or New Zealand tea tree, *L. scoparium*, is a characteristic shrub of Australasia, with prolific flowers and dark green, narrow, aromatic leaves, once used to make bush tea. There are hundreds of cultivars, with red, pink and white flowers. *L. grandiflorum* has more delicate, silvery foliage, and particularly lovely small pale pink flowers. *L. lanigerum*, the woolly tea tree, has grey leaves and distinctive, downy stems, All grow well in poor, acid soils and are drought-tolerant once established.
Height and spread To 4m (12ft)
Hardiness Hardy (borderline) to frost tender Z8–11

Libertia
With elegant, grassy foliage and exquisite, white flowers, these evergreen perennials deserve to be more widely grown. *L. grandiflora* forms a clump 50cm (20in) tall, holding its three-petalled flowers on long stalks in spring. *L. ixioides* is similar, but holds its flowers lower, and has showy yellow seedpods. *L. peregrinans* is smaller (30cm/12in), with tawny leaves with a bright orange mid-rib. The harder you grow it, the brighter the colour will glow. Drought-tolerant.
Height 20–70cm (8–28in)
Hardiness Hardy once established Z9–11

Olearia
DAISY BUSH
Often used for shelter belts in mild, windy climates, such as the Scilly Isles, these foliage shrubs are impressive in flower, smothered in small, white daisies. *O. ilicifolia,* the mountain holly, has crinkly, sharply toothed leaves and prefers some shade. *O. nummularifolia* means 'leaves like coins', which they are. *O. fragrantissima* smells of peaches. Easy and drought-tolerant.
Height and spread 1.2–2.5m (4–8ft)
Hardiness Frost hardy Z9–11

Pittosporum
These evergreen shrubs are grown for the interest of their leaves. Most thrive in coastal areas. (See also page 103.)
Height and spread 6m (20ft) (*P. tenuifolium*)
Hardiness Frost hardy to frost tender Z8–10

Pleurophyllum speciosum
This monster herb, rare in cultivation, has thick oval leaves up to 60cm (2ft) long and 40cm (16in) wide, scored with deep ribs. Flower stalks approach 1m (3ft) in height, and carry heads of pinky-white daisies. Sub-antarctic plant.
Height 1m (3ft); **spread** 1.2m (4ft)
Hardiness Hardy Z7–9

Pseudopanax
LANCEWOOD
With striking juvenile foliage, these are incomparable feature plants, and grow happily in a pot. Most will tolerate sun or shade and a wide range of soils. In its juvenile state, *P. crassifolius* has leathery leaves some 60cm (2ft) long, but only 2cm (¾in) wide, dangling at 45 degrees from a skinny trunk. This stage lasts from 10 to 20 years, when branches begin to develop, the stem thickens and the leaves become shorter and less droopy – making it the quintessential Kiwi tree. The rare toothed lancewood (*P. ferox*) is slower to grow, and needs perfect drainage. *P. laetus* is a pretty shrubby form resembling a strawberry tree (*Arbutus unedo*), but with larger, leathery leaves. Houpara (*P. lessonii*) is hardier, with three-pronged, bright green leaves.
Height To 10m (33ft)
Hardiness Hardy to borderline hardy, apart from *P. laetus*, which is half hardy Z8–11

Tree ferns

Cyathea dealbata
SILVER FERN, PONGA
The national emblem of New Zealand, this is a forest plant that has fronds of shiny green, with undersides of silver. The fronds are rather brittle, so give it a sheltered site, out of the wind, with shade or semi-shade and a moist, humus-rich soil.
Height To 10m (33ft)
Hardiness Half hardy, but will survive outoors in temperatures to -5°C (24°F) with winter protection Z9–11

Cyathea medullaris
MAMAKU, BLACK PONGA
The most common New Zealand tree fern, with a slender trunk and black-stemmed fronds up to 5m (16ft) long – few in number, but very impressive. It will tolerate sunnier sites than the other tree ferns, when given shelter and ample moisture, especially in summer.
Height To 15m (50ft); **spread** 12m (39ft)
Hardiness Half hardy, but will survive outoors in temperatures to -5°C (24°F) with winter protection Z9–11

Dicksonia antarctica
TASMANIAN TREE FERN
Easily grown in damp soil and a sheltered site, this magnificent tree fern has become a horticultural fashion statement, with its fat trunk and huge fronds that reach 2m (6½ft) long. For even bigger fronds, feed occasionally with liquid seaweed feed. Misting and watering the trunk will help it through dry summers, while covering the crown in winter is essential to protect from prolonged frosts.
Height To 15m (49ft); **spread** 4m (13ft)
Hardiness Frost hardy with protection Z9–11

Leptospermum grandiflorum

Libertia peregrinans

Tree fern *Dicksonia antarctica* likes a moist, shady, sheltered spot.

Butia capitata

Arundo donax

Trachycarpus fortunei

Catalpa bignonioides

Jungle plants and flowers that will survive temperate climates

Choose plants with big, bold, beautiful leaves to create a jungle paradise. While palms require full sun, most jungle plants prefer shade and moisture. Some will need winter protection, but most can take dips as low as -10°C (14°F) for short periods.

Palms

Brahea armata
BLUE FAN PALM
This showy Californian palm has large, rigid fans of silver-blue foliage, dangling from a single trunk. It needs good winter drainage and summer moisture, so tends to do best in a pot in full sun.
Height Slowly to 8–10m (26–33ft)
Hardiness Frost hardy Z9–11

Butia capitata
JELLY PALM
The butias are single-stemmed palms from South America, bearing long, pinnate leaves and sweetly scented flowers, followed by round, grape-like, orange fruit. *B. capitata* has a fat, rough trunk and long, blue-grey leaves curving down towards the ground. Happy in sun or shade, it tolerates drought, but will grow larger on moist, fertile soil.
Height and spread Slowly to 7m (23ft)
Hardiness Hardy for short periods to -10°C (14°F) when mature Z9–11

Chamaerops humilis
EUROPEAN FAN PALM
Native to Western Europe, and common in Spain and North Africa, this neat, slow-growing palm with rosettes of fan-shaped leaves prefers sandy, well-drained soil and tolerates drought and wind once established. The blue form, *C. h.* var *cerifera*, also sold as *C. h.* var *argentea*, is narrower in leaf and even slower, but very handsome.
Height and spread To 3m (10ft)
Hardiness Hardy for short periods to -10°C (14°F) grown on well-drained soil in full sun Z9–11

Trachycarpus fortunei
CHUSAN PALM
This rugged palm grows in the mountains of China, Burma and Japan, up to 2,400m (8,000ft), so is perfectly happy in temperate climates in a sheltered site on moist but well drained soil. The trunk, which may

eventually exceed 9m (30ft), is covered in leaf bases, which may be removed to improve its appearance. The fan-shaped, dark green leaves can reach 1m (3ft) across. A miniature version, *T. wagnerianus*, grows to just 3–7m (10–23ft).
Height and spread As above
Hardiness Frost hardy Z8–11

Bamboos and grasses

Arundo donax
GIANT REED
Arundo is prized for its enormous, bamboo-like stems and foliage, which can easily take over your garden. The variegated form, *A. d.* var. *versicolor*, is substantially less rampant, growing to 2.5m (8ft) tall, with white-striped leaves carried either side of stiff stems. For the best foliage, cut to the base annually. The culms of arundo are still used to make reeds for woodwind instruments. Needs moist soil.
Height and spread As above
Hardiness Frost hardy (to -5°C/23°F) Z9–11

Fargesia
Well-behaved, clump-forming, evergreen bamboos ideal for smaller gardens. They like moist soil and full sun, although a few prefer dappled shade. *F. murieliae* has small leaves on arching, yellow-green stems; *F. angustissima* has light, fluffy foliage on red culms; *F. rufa* has an attractive, blue sheen to the foliage, and culms varying from orange to flamingo pink.
Height 3m (10ft); **spread** 1.2m (4ft)
Hardiness Hardy to half hardy Z8–11

Miscanthus sacchariflorus
SILVER BANNER GRASS
This is a stately, upright, strong-growing grass. It has arching, grey-green, strap-like leaves up to 90cm (3ft) long, with silver mid-ribs, and looks splendid grown by water. Cut

back to the ground in late winter before new foliage appears.
Height To 3m (10ft); **spread** Indefinite
Hardiness Frost hardy Z8–11

Phyllostachys
This highly ornamental genus of bamboo needs placing with care in a small garden, as happy clumps will spread laterally once established. Most prefer moist soil in full sun. Black-stemmed *P. nigra*, the oddly knock-kneed *P. aureosulcata* and *P. vivax* 'Aureocaulis' are some of the most attractive. The latter has bright yellow canes randomly striped with green.
Height 2–4m (6½–13ft)
Hardiness Hardy Z7–11

Other foliage plants

Alocasia
ELEPHANT'S EAR
The 70 species of alocasia have large, shield-shaped leaves with deep veining or pleating. Hardy in areas with hotter summers, in summer-cool climes they are usually grown as houseplants, then set outside for the summer. Gold-margined *A. macrorrhiza*, crinkly *A. odora* and handsomely veined *A. sanderiana* make striking summer understorey plants.
Height and spread To 2m (6½ft)
Hardiness Frost tender Z11

Arum italicum
This handsome arum makes a dense, glossy carpet of large, arrow-shaped leaves that cover the ground from late autumn to mid-spring. Then pale green spathes shoot up above the leaves, followed in autumn by a vivid display of red berries. Also known as 'Pictum', the subspecies *italicum* 'Marmoratum' has especially attractive leaves, heavily marbled with cream. Ideal for moist shade under trees and shrubs.
Height 15–30cm (6–12in); **spread** 20–40cm (8–16in)
Hardiness Hardy Z7–11

Catalpa bignonioides
INDIAN BEAN TREE
The huge, pale green, heart-shaped leaves are the chief ornament of this fast-growing tree, which is frequently 'stooled' (cut back) to make them even larger. The mature tree carries purple-white flowers followed by long, dangling, black seedpods. There is a yellow ('Aurea') and a variegated

('Variegata') form, both smaller than the species.
Height 15m (50ft); **spread** 8m (26ft)
Hardiness Hardy Z8–11

Cotinus 'Grace'
SMOKE BUSH
This variety of smoke bush is a vigorous shrub with larger than usual oval leaves that are ruby red when young, darkening to a sultry burgundy by summer, and flushing orange before dropping. It responds well to 'stooling', helping to contain its sprawling habit.
Height and spread 3–6m (10–20ft)
Hardiness Hardy Z7–11

Fatsia japonica
FALSE CASTOR OIL PLANT
This evergreen shrub deserves a place in every garden, growing well in part sun and deep shade, and seeming to thrive on neglect. In addition to its dramatically architectural, deep green, polished leaves, it produces sculptural, creamy flowerheads through the winter, followed by small, black fruit. Variegated forms are available – ignore them.
Height and spread 4m (13ft)
Hardiness Hardy Z8–11

Magnolia grandiflora
This beautiful tree, often grown as a wall shrub, is valuable both for its large, shiny, evergreen leaves, and its huge, highly scented summer flowers. 'Exmouth' is a fine variety, with leaves glossy on the upper side, but with a rusty, suede-like coating beneath. It will cover a house if left unchecked, but responds well to pruning.
Height and spread 10m (33ft)
Hardiness Hardy Z8–11

Paulownia tomentosa
FOXGLOVE TREE
A fast-growing, spreading, deciduous tree, with large, soft, plate-like, mid-green leaves, followed by a profusion of lilac-pink flowers in summer. The tree is frequently 'stooled', sacrificing the flowers to make the leaves bigger, and restricting its size to 2–3m (6½–10ft).
Height 15m (50ft); **spread** 9m (30ft)
Hardiness Hardy Z8–11

Sambucus
ELDER
Elders are generally grown for their ornamental foliage colours, and there are very many to choose from. The coloured forms of *S. nigra* (the common elder native to Europe) are very vigorous. 'Aurea' is golden yellow, while 'Guincho Purple' has green leaves, which darken to purple-black. Finer in form are the *S. racemosa* varieties, with feathery, acer-like foliage. 'Plumosa Aurea' is golden, while the aptly named 'Black Lace' is deep purple. Elders generally do best in sun and moist, fertile soil, but are not at all picky. 'Plumosa Aurea', however, is best placed in light shade to prevent the sun scorching the foliage.
Height and spread 4m (13ft)
Hardiness Hardy Z7–11

Flowers

Brugmansia
ANGEL'S TRUMPET
An evergreen shrub from the Andes, with smooth, berry-like fruits (as opposed to the dry, prickly capsules of closely related *Datura*). Brugmansia is easy to grow in moist, humus-rich soil. Most cultivars have been produced from a hybrid, *B.* x *candida*, and have large, dangling, trumpet-shaped flowers in shades of pink, yellow, orange or white. While it prefers sun, variegated forms should be given light shade to prevent the foliage scorching.
Height and spread 3–5m (10–16ft)
Hardiness Half hardy to frost tender Z10–11

Dahlia
A tuberous rooted member of the daisy family, native to Central America, dahlias are back in fashion, especially cultivars with dark or bronzy leaves such as 'Moonfire' or the popular 'Bishop' series. Stake well, feed generously and deadhead regularly.
Height and spread 1–2m (3–6ft)
Hardiness Half hardy to frost tender Z10–11

Roscoea
These small, orchid-flowered gingers originate in the Himalayas or Sichuan, and are more tolerant of cold than their taller cousins. Preferring cool, dappled shade in humus-rich, moisture-retentive but well-drained soil, they are excellent beneath the canopy of a jungle giant. Plant as bulbs in spring for them to flower in summer. All are exquisite, *R. cautleyoides* and its hybrid *R.* 'Beesiana' perhaps the loveliest.
Height and spread 15–40cm (6–16in)
Hardiness Hardy to frost hardy Z8–11

Brugmansia sanguinea will lose its leaves in cooler conditions.

Tithonia rotundifolia
MEXICAN SUNFLOWER
In its native Mexico, this sun-loving annual will make 2m (6½ft), but in cooler climes stops at around 1.2m (4ft), forming a neat, floriferous plant producing vivid daisy flowers all summer. 'Torch' is a luminous orange, 'Goldfinger' has larger, softer-coloured flowers, while 'Fiesta del Sol' has dazzling blooms 7cm (2¾in) across.
Height and spread As above
Hardiness Half hardy Z10–11

Zantedeschia
ARUM LILY, CALLA LILY
Curiously, zantedeschias are botanically neither arums nor lilies. But they are superb garden plants, with lush clumps of arrow-shaped leaves and dramatic, waxy spathes. Moisture-loving *Z. aethiopica* has two outstanding cultivars, snowy white 'Crowborough' and green and white 'Green Goddess', both hardy to -8°C (18°F). The multi-coloured calla hybrids, often with spotty leaves, are only half-hardy, but make a summer splash in the jungle garden.
Height and spread 45cm–1m (1½–3ft)
Hardiness Hardy to frost tender Z8–11

Tithonia rotundifolia 'Goldfinger'

Zantedeschia aethiopica

Carpobrotus edulis

Kalanchoe beharensis

Tough and adaptable desert plants

You cannot help but admire desert plants, for their sheer determination to survive. Many are also remarkably striking. While US hardiness zones are given, all these plants can withstand at least 1°C (30°F) of overnight frost, especially if kept dry.

Carpobrotus edulis
HOTTENTOT FIG
A small, creeping succulent, which does not grow very tall, but spreads indefinitely. It has bright yellow, daisy flowers from late spring to summer.
Height 15cm (6in); **spread** Indefinite
Hardiness Frost tender Z10–11

Echeveria
There are over 150 species of *Echeveria* – small succulent herbs with pink, orange or yellow flowers carried on delicate, single-branched stalks above beautiful rosettes of symmetrically arranged leaves. They are native to the rocky hillsides of Mexico, Venezuela and Peru, where many grow in shady, pine-oak woodland, making them well adapted for growing in cooler climates.
E. secunda var. *glauca*, with its fat, blue-grey leaves, is the most common form, but there are many attractive hybrids, including shiny pink *E.* 'Perle d'Azur' and *E. runyonii* 'Topsey Turvey', resembling tiny grey shoe horns.
Height and spread 5–30cm (2–12in)
Hardiness Z9–11

Echinocactus grusonii
GOLDEN BARREL CACTUS
One of the most popular cacti, the golden barrel cactus is grown for its large, rounded form, embellished with parallel rows of clustered, golden spines. Golden yellow flowers are produced a few at a time, emerging from the large patch of wool at the plant's centre. In their natural habitat in Mexico, plants may remain single or produce plantlets to form a clump.
Height 1.5m (4ft); **spread** 1m (3ft)
Hardiness Frost tender Z10–11

Encelia farinosa
BRITTLEBRUSH
This silver-leaved desert shrub native to north-western Mexico and the south-western United States has woolly, silver leaves, and orangey-yellow, daisy flowers borne on slender stems in spring.
Height To 1m (3ft)
Hardiness Frost tender Z10–11

Fouquieria
OCOTILLO, BOOJUM
The genus *Fouquieria* comprises seven species of succulent trees and shrubs originating in Mexico and southern parts of the adjacent USA.
F. splendens, the ocotillo, has sparse, upright stems growing as high as 7m (23ft), densely set with spines. Stiff, red tubular flowers are borne along the tips in spring and summer. It is an intriguing, highly architectural plant. The boojum or cirio (*F. columnaris*) is a mysterious dinosaur of a plant, consisting of a carrot-like stem sprouting short, twiggy branches along its length. It is hideous, but fascinating.
Height 2.5–9m (8–30ft); **spread** 3–4.5m (10–15ft)
Hardiness Frost tender Z10–11

Kalanchoe
Like the echeverias, *Kalanchoe* is part of the Crassulaceae family. Some are grown as flowering houseplants, others for their distinctive foliage, which can be attractively scalloped, as in *K. marmorata*, while *K. beharensis* varieties have almost triangular felty leaves. 'Fang' has curious teeth on the leaf underside. Many species, like *K. delagoensis*, employ a remarkable form of vegetative propagation: a bracelet of tiny, rooted plantlets grows up around the edges of the leaf. In nature, these fall off during dry periods, and root and grow in the soil – but gardeners can simply pot them up.
Height and spread 10–30cm (4–12in)
Hardiness Frost tender Z10–11

Lampranthus
This colourful groundcover succulent from South Africa now thrives as far afield as south-west England, where it is ideal for covering walls and dry, rocky banks. Large mats of foliage are covered with brightly coloured daisy flowers in hot shades. To give of their best, they need a little water in winter, none at all in summer. *L. saturatus* (magenta), *L. roseus* (pink), *L. haworthii* (mauve) and *L. aureus* (orange/red) are all floriferous, and grow easily from cuttings.
Height 10cm (4in); **spread** indefinite
Hardiness Frost tender Z10–11

Opuntia
PRICKLY PEAR
Native to the warmer regions of Central, North and South America and the West Indies, prickly pears have naturalized in arid areas throughout the world, and are now a serious weed in parts of the Himalayas. They are the most distinctive of cacti, characterized by thick, flat stems (often mistaken for leaves), divided into oval pads. Depending on the species, they can form small clusters, like the pretty, pink-flowered *O. basilaris*, or branching shrubs (*O. ellisiana*), or trees (*O. tomentosa*). In contrast to the flat-stemmed species are the chollas, with jointed, cylindrical stems and fiendish spines. Many produce a juicy edible fruit, while the new stems of *O. ficus-indica* are popular as salad vegetables and pickles.
Height and spread To 4m (13ft)
Hardiness Hardy to frost tender Z10

Echinocactus grusonii needs bright light and a dry atmosphere to thrive.

Useful addresses

AUSTRALIA

Frogmore Gardens
Blackwood Rd, Newbury, VIC 3458
www.frogmoregardens.com.au
Nursery and display gardens

Greywater for Gardens
10 Plumtree Rise, Croydon Hills,
Melbourne, VIC 3136
www.greywaterforgardens.com
Greywater and irrigation systems

Lifestyle Gardens
167 Gilbert St, Latrobe, TAS 7307
www.lifestylegardens.com.au
Nursery and garden supplies

Provincial Native Plants
www.provincialnativeplants.com.au

Quambay Nursery
Tel: 03 5455 1367
www.quambynursery.com.au

CANADA

David Hunter Garden Centers
2084 West Broadway,
Vancouver, BC, V6J 1Z4
www.davidhuntergardencenters.com

Garden of Eden Tree Farm
P.O. Box 20, 9594 Somers Road
Eden, ON, N0J 1H0; Tel: 519-866-5269
www.amtelecom.net/~edentree
Shrubs, ferns, evergreens and trees

Golden Bough Tree Farm
900 Napanee Road, Marlbank, ON,
K0K 2L0; www.goldenboughtrees.ca
Rare and native plants

Plants of Perfection
Langley, BC; CristinaH@telus.net
www.plantsofperfection.com
Rare, unusual and tropical plants

NEW ZEALAND

Naja Garden Centre
198 Molesworth Drive, Mangawhai
Heads 0505; www.najagarden.co.nz
Coastal plants

Sunny Lady Organic Gardens
30 Annan Grove, Papakowhai, Porirua
City, Wellington; www.sunnylady.co.nz
Environmentally friendly products

Taupo Native Plant Nursery
155 Centennial Drive, Taupo, Waikato
3378; www.tauponativeplant.co.nz

The Tree Place Ltd
56 Panorama Road, Mount Wellington,
Auckland City, Auckland
www.thetreeplace.co.nz
Semi-mature trees

SOUTH AFRICA

**Indigenous Bulb Association of South
Africa**, PO Box 12265,
N1 City 7463; www.newplant.co.za

Petal Faire
131 Allcock Street, Colbyn, Pretoria
0083; www.petalfaire.co.za
Exotic and indigenous plants

Riverside Garden Centre
490 Riverside Rd, Umgeni Park,
Durban; www.riversidegardencentre.co.za
Nursery and landscape service

UNITED KINGDOM

Abbotsbury Subtropical Gardens
Abbotsbury, Nr Weymouth,
Dorset DT3 4LA
www.abbotsbury-tourism.co.uk/gardens

Adur Gardening
www.adurgardening.com
Pots and plants

Bellamont Topiary
Long Bredy, Dorset DT2 9HN
www.bellamont-topiary.co.uk

The British Cactus Society
membership@bcss.org.uk

David Austin Roses
Bowling Green Lane, Albrighton,
Wolverhampton WV7 3HB
www.davidaustinroses.com

Desert to Jungle
Henlade Garden Nursery
Lower Henlade, Taunton TA3 5NB
www.deserttojungle.com
Hardy exotic and architectural plants

Duchy of Cornwall Nursery
Lostwithiel, Cornwall PL22 0HW
www.duchyofcornwallnursery.co.uk
Over 4000 varieties of plants

Knoll Gardens
Hampreston, Wimborne, Dorset BH21
7ND; www.knollgardens.co.uk
Specialists in ornamental grasses

Guy Furner
Woodlanders, Manor Farm Yard,
Symondsbury, Bridport, Dorset DT6 6HQ
Woodcraft and garden design

Franchi Sementi Seeds of Italy
www.seedsofitaly.com

Kevin Nunn
Hall Nunn, 202 Gerrards Green,
Beaminster, Dorset DT8 3ED
Garden landscaping

Keanegardeneur
PO Box 44355, London SW20 OXB
www.keanegardeneur.co.uk
Garden gloves

Sankey
Bennerly Road, Bulwell, Nottingham
NG6 8PE; www.rsankey.com
Composters and water butts

Thompson & Morgan (UK) Ltd
Poplar Lane, Ipswich, Suffolk IP8 3BU
www.Thompson-Morgan.com
Plants and seeds

Westcrete
Stoney Bridges, Axminster, Devon
EX13 5RL; www.westcrete-ltd.co.uk
Landscaping and building materials

UNITED STATES

Aldrich Berry Farm & Nursery
190 Aldrich Road, Mossyrock, WA
98564; www.plantnative.com

Caldwell Nursery
2436 Band Road, Rosenberg, TX
77471; www.caldwellhort.com

GrowOrganic.com
P.O. Box 2209, 125 Clydesdale Court,
Grass Valley, CA 95945
www.groworganic.com

High Country Gardens
2902 Rufina Street, Santa Fe, NM 87
www.highcountrygardens.com
Supplies, including waterwise plants

Lukas Nursery
1909 Slavia Road, Oviedo, Florida
32765; www.lukasnursery.com
Landscape, patio and indoor plants

Pack's Nursery
754 Pack Rd, Boaz, AL; packsnursery.com
Hollies and boxwoods

Portland Nursery
5050 SE Stark, Portland, OR 97215
www.portlandnursery.com

Stokes Tropicals
4806 E. Old Spanish Trail, Jeanerette,
LA 70544; stokestropicals.com

Lampranthus haworthii

Opuntia microdasys

Fouquieria columnaris

Echeveria runyonii

Index

Plant hardiness zones

Plant entries in the directory of this book have been given hardiness descriptions and zone numbers. Hardiness definitions are as follows:

Frost tender
A plant which needs heated greenhouse protection through the winter in the local area. May be damaged by temperatures below 5°C (41°F).

Half hardy
A plant which cannot be grown outside during the colder months in the local area and needs greenhouse protection through the winter. Can withstand temperatures down to 0°C (32°F).

Frost hardy
A plant which, when planted outside, will survive through milder winters in the local area, with additional protection. Can withstand temperatures down to -5°C (23°F).

Fully hardy
A plant which, when planted outside, will survive reliably through the winter in the local area. Can withstand temperatures down to -15°C (5°F).

There is widespread use of the zone number system to express the hardiness of many plant species and cultivars. The zonal system used, shown below, was developed by the Agricultural Research Service of the United States Department of Agriculture. According to this system, there are 11 zones in total, based on the average annual minimum temperature in a particular geographical zone.

The zone rating for each plant indicates the coldest zone in which a correctly planted subject can survive the winter. Where a plant's hardiness is borderline, the first number indicates the marginal zone and the second the safer zone.

This is not a hard and fast system, but simply a rough indicator, as many factors other than temperature also play an important part where hardiness is concerned. These factors include altitude, wind exposure, proximity to water, soil type, the presence of snow or shade, night temperature, and the amount of water received by a plant. These kinds of factors can easily alter a plant's hardiness by as much as two zones. The presence of long-term snow cover in the winter especially can allow plants to survive in colder zones.

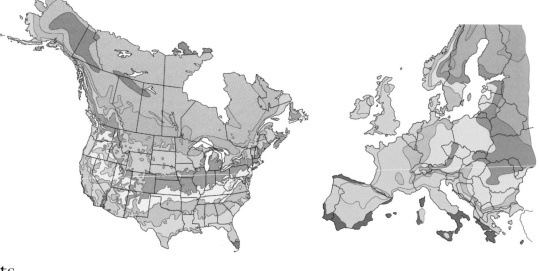

Zone 1 Below -45°C (-50°F)
Zone 2 -45 to -40°C (-50 to -40°F)
Zone 3 -40 to -34°C (-40 to -30°F)
Zone 4 -34 to -29°C (-30 to -20°F)
Zone 5 -29 to -23°C (-20 to -10°F)
Zone 6 -23 to -18°C (-10 to 0°F)
Zone 7 -18 to -12°C (0 to 10°F)
Zone 8 -12 to -7°C (10 to 20°F)
Zone 9 -7 to -1°C (20 to 30°F)
Zone 10 -1 to 4°C (30 to 40°F)
Zone 11 Above 4°C (40°F)

Acknowledgements

Publisher's acknowledgements

The publishers would like to thank the following for generously allowing the use of their gardens for photography:
Abbey Gardens, Tresco, Scilly Isles; Abbotsbury Subtropical Gardens, Nr Weymouth, Dorset DT3 4LA; Beth Chatto Gardens, Elmstead Market, Colchester, Essex CO7 7DB; Capel Manor, Enfield, Middlesex EN1 4RQ; Frances Franklin, 4 Fernlea Road, Burnham on Sea, Essex CM0 8EJ; Tracey Leverett, RHS Garden Hyde Hall, Rettendon, Chelmsford CM3 8ET; Iford Manor, Bradford on Avon, Wiltshire BA15 2BA; Mike Evans, Shillingstone, Dorset; Nigel Buckie, London; The Garden House, Buckland Monachorum, Yelverton, Devon PL20 7LQ; Derek Jarman's garden, Prospect Cottage, Dungeness, Kent; and Huntington Botanical Gardens, Los Angeles.
The publishers would also like to thank the following agencies and individuals for permission to reproduce their images:

Alamy: p12 Alex Ramsay; p13l Bildarchiv Monheim GmbH; p62mr Barry Mason; **Gap Photos:** p14 S&O; p27l, p94 Rob Whitworth; p42l, p69l (design Shunmyo Masuno), p86r, 87 Jerry Harpur; p71l Jonathan Need; p77bl Dianna Jazwinski; p80 Clive Nichols; p81br, p102 Ron Evans; p90l Gerry Whitmont; p106 John Glover; p108l Adrian Bloom; p120bl Richard Bloom; p142, 143 Howard Rice; p143 2nd top J. S. Sira; **Garden Picture Library:** p18l; p33 ml Juliette H. Wade; p49br Chris Burrows; **Amy Christian:** p24, p29r; **Corbis:** p26l Kevin R. Morris; p26r Philip de Bay/Historical Picture Archive; **Felicity Forster:** p59; **istock:** p27r, p33tl, p33tr, p46r; **Lynn Keddie:** p33b, p74r; **Helen Dillon:** p34b; **Fernando Cordero/De Yturbe Arquitectos:** p41 (www.deyturbe.com); **Claire Rae:** p61r, p67l, p70l, p75l; **Eric J. Gouda/ Utrecht Botanic Gardens:** p73t; **Tim Sandall/ RHS The Garden:** p73 bl & r; **Marion Brenner:** p114r, 116l; **Will Giles:** p126r; **Jerry Harpur:** p128r.

Author's acknowledgements

Warmest thanks to the many people who have shared their expertise in the making of this book, and patiently submitted to trial by photography: Guy Furner and Kevin Nunn, who built our rill, thyme pavement and spectacular dry river bed; Rob Gudge and Dave Root of Desert to Jungle, for sharing their secrets of successful overwintering, and letting us loose on their treasure house of exotic plants; Eyre and Harriet Sykes, for so generously sharing their beautiful topiary, their expertise and their garden.

Also thanks to Jenny Waterhouse for her invaluable advice on design and all her many kindnesses; to Frances Franklin, for her many helpful suggestions; to Gary Povey, master of the hose; to Brendan Connolly for the loan of his beautiful lanterns; to Keith Auckland, for his support over a far longer time than was ever anticipated; and above all to Lynn Keddie, for her superb pictures, and unfailing solidarity, patience and humour.